MW00983895

Tito Santana's
Tales from the Ring

Best Wishes To
Dave
From
Tito Santana
Hall of Fame 2004

Tito Santana
with Tom Caiazzo

Thanks for being A fan!

SPORTS PUBLISHING L.L.C.

SportsPublishingLLC.com

ISBN 13: 978-1-59670-325-4

Publishers: Peter L. Bannon and Joseph J. Bannon Sr.
Senior managing editor: Susan M. Moyer
Editor: Doug Hoepker
Art director: Dustin J. Hubbart

Sports Publishing L.L.C.
804 North Neil Street
Champaign, IL 61820
Phone: 1-877-424-2665
Fax: 217-363-2073
www.SportsPublishingLLC.com

Printed in the United States of America

Library of Congress information available upon request

To my lovely mother Juanita, beautiful wife Leah, and my precious sons Michael, Matthew, and Mark. All of you have been an inspiration and the loves of my life.

CONTENTS

FOREWORD
BY SGT. SLAUGHTER

At-ten-hut! Okay, at ease and listen up.

From its inception, professional wrestling was created to orchestrate good versus evil in the combat zone of the squared circle, to pit the beloved hero against the wicked villain. A hero in professional wrestling is that character who performs with remarkable bravery and exceptional nobility, and with great strength and courage. A warrior of distinguished valor, a hero is admired for his outstanding qualities and achievements. Fans believe that hero can accomplish anything. He cannot lose, but if he does, it's because the injurious villain or villains used some dastardly, underhanded deed to escape certain defeat.

In the 35 years that I have participated in the squared circle of sports entertainment, I was both a villain and a hero, of course having more fun and satisfaction portraying the wicked villain. But there have only been an elite handful of *beloved* heroes. The ability of a wrestling hero to produce and elevate an act of simulated and passionate suffering by using body and facial expressions, is slowly becoming a lost art in the world of sports entertainment today. One of the all time greatest beloved heroes that I ever had the privilege and honor to story tell with was Tito Santana.

Tito Santana was what we term in professional wrestling as a "night off." That may not sound like a compliment, but it is an elite one. Those two words put you in an elite class that not only makes you feel appreciated at the 55-minute mark of a 60-minute match, but it puts you in a very high demand with the sport's most astute, consummate, and creative-minded talents in our glorious sport, especially the artistic ring general and those wicked villains. One of Tito's biggest assets in his gifted arsenal was his capability to make the timely resurgence in a match, with so much fire, energy, determination, and ability to bring the exhilarated audience right along with him. That is what put Tito Santana in a league of his own and one of the many reasons for his tremendous success in professional wrestling.

Tito's fan base and popularity around the world is legendary. At one time in Tito's career, Vince McMahon, the owner and genius behind the amazing success of the WWE, once told me that Tito Santana was so popular that he received three times the amount of fan mail than any other superstar in the WWE! Not too bad for someone who never held the WWE World Heavyweight Championship.

Tito is my friend and it was always a thrill and a joy to step into the squared circle with him, entertaining all the millions of fans around the world. We also shared a very special and respectful admiration for each other right from our first introduction by a revered and mutual friend, Don Kernolde, one of the most creative minds ever in our celebrated business. I will forevermore treasure and value our friendship. He is a legend in the illustrious world of sports entertainment and it was a distinguished honor to be inducted with him in 2004 into the WWE Hall of Fame.

Any questions, maggot? Good, then until we meet again: YOU'RE DISMISSED! Carry on . . .

Sgt. Slaughter
April 29, 2008

FOREWORD
BY "MR. WONDERFUL," PAUL ORNDORFF

I first met Tito when we worked together for Eddie Graham in the Florida territory. He had started a few months before me. But I really got to know Tito later on when we were part of the Georgia territory. Because we were both former college and professional football players, we bonded immediately. He had a passion for competition and a spirit that was unmatched. Unlike others, Tito was honest and straightforward. He would tell you exactly what he was willing to do and what he wasn't. As time went on, we became very close friends and could always count on each other.

After leaving Georgia, Tito and I both went to work for Vince McMahon and the WWF. Although other guys initially were getting the push, neither Tito nor I were going to be denied. He was very talented; he wasn't going to be held back. He was a very unselfish person in the ring and had tremendous psychology. Some of best wrestling matches I ever had—and I mean matches that went thirty to sixty minutes long—were with Tito Santana. We had a passion for the business and we worked our butts off in the ring. We would always steal the show. We knew how to work, how to control the crowd, and how to get the people right where we wanted them.

In fact, when Tito and I first started with the WWF, we wrestled for thirty minutes in Kansas City. Vince McMahon Jr. was at ringside and after the match he came into the locker room and said, "That was the best wrestling match I ever saw!" I can say without reservation that Tito was one of the best workers ever in the business.

Tito was and is also a great person outside the ring. He never stabbed anyone in the back and everybody liked Tito. If you every needed anything he would be the first one to help you out. Tito is the kind of guy that I would be proud of to have as my son. And I mean that.

–Paul Orndorff, December 23, 2007

INTRODUCTION
BY TITO SANTANA

For a long time my life pursuit was wrestling. I spent most of my career with the World Wrestling Federation, from 1979-1980 and then again from 1983-1993. I reached the top of the sport as a two-time Intercontinental champion, a two-time World Tag-Team champion, and in 1989 the "King of the Ring." Along with only Hulk Hogan, I competed at each of the first nine WrestleMania events. For my accomplishments, I was inducted into the WWF Hall of Fame in 2004. That's not too shabby for someone who was often deliberately called "Chico Santana" by former professional wrestler and governor of Minnesota, Jesse Ventura.

I love professional wrestling and I still perform in the ring at 54 years young. I do it because of the fans, whom I want to thank for their support over the years. I wouldn't be where I am today without my fans. They've given so much to me that I want to return the favor and share with them the story of my life. That story isn't complete without an introduction to my life before I first stepped into a ring.

I was born in 1953 in Mission, Texas, a small city located about 250 miles south of San Antonio and 70 miles west of the Gulf of Mexico. The city is at the southern tip of the state, about five miles from the Mexican border. I grew up in the Rio Grande Valley, a tropical area where about 90 percent of the people were Mexican and farming was the main industry. My parents, like most of the residents of Mission, were migrant farm workers. They married when my mother, Juanita Cavazos Solis, was 30 years old and my father, Merced Solis, was 31. My mom's family was pretty well off—her parents owned an entire block of houses in Mission that he rented out—but my dad came from a family of poor farm laborers.

I had three sisters, Viola, Belia, and Dalia, and one brother, Roberto. Dalia was born with cystic fibrosis and died before she was a year old. My Dad wanted a big family that he could put to work in the fields. We lived in a small, two-bedroom house given to us by my mother's parents. My brother and I shared a bed with my dad, and my two sisters shared a bed with my mom. For most of my childhood, I never lived in a house that had running water. But Mom kept the house immaculate and stayed busy ironing our clothes and fixing us three home-cooked meals a day.

My cheerful mother, herself the oldest of 16 kids, held our family together. I remember kissing her often as a child and comparing our love to that of little parakeets, like the ones my grandmother kept as pets. She was very strict while my siblings and I were growing up, and made sure we didn't veer off course too much. She was never shy about speaking her mind, and was straightforward and to the point.

I wasn't a perfect son for her to raise. In fifth grade, I started hanging around with a group of kids that Mom didn't like, and I refused to quit spending time with them.

Finally, she told me that since I wouldn't listen, she had called a reform school and had enrolled me; I was to pack my belongings because they were coming to pick me up after supper. She actually dressed me up and packed an old suitcase for me, then made me sit and wait for whoever was coming. That hour I spent waiting seemed like days. I sweated profusely, thinking I was a goner. When no one showed up, Mom told me they must have gotten lost, so I might as well go to bed. She said it so calmly that I believed her. Needless to say, I wasted no time the next day and found new friends who would meet my mother's approval.

My father was a big man with broad shoulders, about 6-foot-1 and 220 pounds. He was a very handsome man whose family came from Spain. He had a light complexion and always wore a Stetson cowboy hat and boots. In contrast to my mom, my dad wasn't around much, especially on the weekends. He drank very little but used to frequent the local cantinas to socialize with women and dance. He also enjoyed playing pool at the local pool halls. On many occasions he told the family that he was taking us out for dinner. We would get dressed up and await his return, but he would not be back until early the next morning. My poor mom would confront him verbally, but he would never answer her. He would never admit to anything my mother accused him of; instead, he would respond with silence. It was just his way. I remember Mom explaining to us once, when we asked where Dad was, that on Fridays my dad would park his truck at the Mexican border, take a cab across the border, and not return until Monday morning. Despite his social lifestyle, however, Dad was still a good provider for his family. But there is no doubt that he was a horrible husband.

Like most other migrant kids at our school, we would miss the first six weeks and the last six weeks of the school year because of work. The school system had after-school programs to help us catch up. That's how we got promoted from grade to grade each year despite missing so much class time. The routine for my family was always the same: first we went to Milford, Illinois, to pick asparagus; from there we moved to Wisconsin or Michigan to pick cherries or strawberries; in early September we would move to Indiana to pick tomatoes and we stayed there until the middle of October or until the frost ruined the tomato crop. During the Christmas holidays we would pick oranges, grapefruits, or carrots. When March came around, we would pick onions after school and on weekends.

The very first trip I remember taking as a migrant worker was when I was six. In the middle of April, my siblings and I were pulled out of school. We were very excited as we packed our 1956 blue and white Chevy Bel Air, which my dad had purchased brand new. As we got ready for the road trip, my grandparents, who lived next door, gave Mom $20 to pay for food for us kids. It was our first trip as a family. Little did I know that traveling would become a way of life and that our summer vacations from school would always be spent working.

We arrived in Milford after two and a half days of driving and settled in our new home, aluminum barracks set up next to a dairy farm. I'll never forget the smell of the cow manure dense in the air. The rooms were small with no inside facilities at all, just an aluminum wall separating us from our neighbors on both sides. But we each had a bed, and the room was also equipped with a small gas stove and a small refrigerator. We made do, with Mom always laying fresh mouse traps upon arrival.

At seven o'clock the next morning we began our day alongside over 150 migrant workers. My brothers and sisters and I were excited about working with our parents. In the field, Dad held out a stalk of asparagus and gave us our instructions. "I just finished talking to the boss," he told us. "This is the size of asparagus we want in the baskets." Asparagus was new to us. The vegetable grew from the ground up, and we would break it off, leaving behind a couple of inches. The smaller asparagus was left behind for future picking.

My mother always called me by my nickname, "Nuné," which means Junior in Spanish. "Nuné," she said to me, "you come with me and help me fill my basket. Belia, you go with your dad." Mom glanced quickly upward and added, "May the good Lord help us." She would always say that every time we went out to the fields.

My dad and mom were not slave drivers. They let us work at our own pace. Dad would tell us things like, "We'll work for an hour and then we'll stop to eat breakfast." It was an attainable goal that kept us working without complaining. Mom made breakfast at eight o'clock in the morning, lunch around noon, and a smaller meal around four in the afternoon. We ate as a group usually on the ground, picnic style. We always ended our meals with Dad saying, "Ready? Full stomach, happy heart, let's go back to work!" We usually worked until six o'clock in the evening.

Every night, after Mom finished feeding us, she'd heat a bucket of water and bathe all four of us kids. We did a lot of bonding, living so close together and in foreign parts of the country.

———

There is so much to learn in life, especially when growing up as a minority. Certain things can only be learned by experience. In that way, I was introduced to prejudice the hard way. I knew I was different from most folks from my travels far from home. When we would head to the northern states to work as migrants, we sometimes traveled in the back of a truck as if we were all crowded into a covered wagon. I didn't hate what I was, or who I was. I just couldn't understand why some people would stare at us when we would stop to eat at a truck stop. I can't say I heard any laughter or snide remarks from onlookers, but the stares alone cut pretty deep. I wanted something better for all of us.

My first serious experience with prejudice did not come about because of race, but because of class. I fell in love in tenth grade with Carmen, a Mexican girl who came from a well-to-do family in town. Her father was a doctor and her mother worked at her family's business. She invited me over to her house my sophomore year of high school. While I was waiting for her to get ready to go to a movie, I was questioned by her grandfather. He wanted to know all about my family. Since I was poor and her family was affluent, I was embarrassed by some of my answers. But at least I was honest. The next day at school, Carmen told me her family did not want us to see each other any more. Still, we dated for two years behind her parents' backs.

Throughout high school, I experienced discrimination. I was called Mexican in a derogatory sense by some of my white friends. It bothered me at first, but I learned to tell which comments were harmless and which ones were intended to hurt me. I got into a few fistfights because of the name-calling. I had a short temper, which I eventually grew out of as I became an adult.

This early adversity helped shape me into the person and professional I eventually became. I later learned that through sports, I could help overcome such petty treatment and fit in. In eighth grade, I met my future football coach, Louis Sanchez, a big man who had been an All-America catcher on the University of Texas baseball team. One day during P.E., he called me into his office during the middle of class. "How would you like to go out for football, son?" he asked me. "I can see a lot of potential in you."

I was speechless and caught completely by surprise. I knew nothing about organized football. I thought a player had to pay for his own equipment, and I knew Mom wouldn't go for that. We worked too hard for our money to spend it on a luxury item like football equipment. I also knew some of the other guys had already been playing for two years and were significantly more experienced than me. Not to mention the players were huge and muscular. I was intimidated by them.

So I told Coach Sanchez, "I'll have to ask my mother. I

don't think she will go for it. In fact, I think she would be totally against it, Coach."

"Tell your mother that I will even drive you home after practice," Coach added, trying to sweeten the pot.

The next day Coach Sanchez was waiting for my answer. I hadn't even bothered to ask Mom because I was too scared to play. I told Coach that my mother wouldn't allow it. But I guess he knew from my expression that I was lying. He just smiled and asked me to consider playing the next year.

Later on that year, Coach Sanchez held basketball tryouts. Even though I'd never played, I decided to try out for the team. This time around, I had some incentive for trying something new. Our school had an after-school study hall program for migrant students. Supposedly the program was designed to help us catch up for the weeks we missed; but as far as I was concerned, the migrant students were being singled out and punished. I hated it. So, along with my friend Louis Ortega, I tried out for the basketball team in hopes of being exempt from the study hall program.

"You can try out," coach told me, "but I've got all my starters coming back. We were undefeated last year, so I can't guarantee you anything."

"That's good enough for me—all I want is a chance," I replied.

I made good on that opportunity and made the cut, but poor Louis had to go back to study hall. That began my athletic career. During my junior and senior years in high school, I played basketball and football and enjoyed my time as an athlete. I couldn't believe the strides that I had made both on the football field and on the basketball court. Unlike others who worked out year round and went to camps in the summer, I did none of that, needing to work in the fields to support my family. I can attribute my rise in sports to having natural athletic ability. The Lord was clearly guiding me.

I played very well in football my senior year, starting at running back and strong safety. From a statistical standpoint, I did even better in basketball, averaging 27.9 points per game as a 6-foot-2 center going up against guys who were two to six inches taller. Even though I did great on the court, my team had a losing season and it was difficult for me to attract attention from college scouts. I only received one basketball scholarship offer from San Marcos.

We had a losing season in football, too, but I was good enough to be recruited. Two schools offered me football scholarships, West Texas State and again San Marcos. Seeing that football was the best opportunity for me to get an education, I accepted the full-ride offer from West Texas State.

———

I picked West Texas State in part because it was farther from home than San Marcos. By my senior year, my dad and mom were on the verge of divorce. He was making life for my mom miserable. My two sisters had gotten married young, likely just to get out of the house. I also wanted to get as far away as possible. So West Texas, in the Panhandle town of Canyon, was my destination.

In 1971, when I started college, West Texas had around 6,600 students. It was noted for its business education program, but my major was physical education. Unlike Mission, the city of Canyon was flat and almost desert-like. The area was notorious for sandstorms and tornadoes and it got quite cold there. My freshman year, I saw snow for the first time in my life.

College was a piece of cake for me. I had no real trouble making the adjustment, and soon I was getting the education that I had always wanted—and it was free. I loved playing football, so my "job" was fun. All I had to do was play football and go to school. College was the greatest time of my life. I was getting by on the $250 I had in the bank, plus the $15 a month I was given for laundry money as part of my scholarship. Room and board was covered, and I found that if I needed some extra spending cash I could make $10 a semester by donating a pint of my blood.

I was pretty naive about the entire educational process. I had no idea that in college I only had to go to class on certain days of the week. Many of my teammates on the football team didn't bother to go to classes. But I liked attending class and took my education more seriously. Besides, going to class gave me a chance to mingle with pretty girls on campus.

The opening day of football practice presented me with another first: black teammates. In Mission, I had been surrounded by mostly Latinos and Anglos. It wasn't until I arrived at West Texas that I had my first regular contact with blacks. We all got along well, just as I had done in high school when many of my teammates were white.

Practice started out easy. We were weighed and measured, then we went out and ran around the track for 12 minutes. The coaches wanted to see what kind of shape we were in. I had been running for two weeks prior, so I did pretty well, coming in fifth out of 60 players. After our run we had a meeting to go over some of the plays that we would be working on that afternoon. At the meeting, I found out that I was going to play tight end on offense and linebacker on defense. I wasn't disappointed to learn that I was fourth on the depth chart at tight end; at the time everyone around me looked pretty confident and I was worried that I wouldn't be able to play much. Afternoon practice began and after watching some of my teammates I got a boost in confidence. I quickly realized that I was capable of competing for a starting position, even though I was trying out for different positions than what I had played in high school.

I really wanted to play on defense because I enjoyed the physicality of the position, but I never got a chance. By the end of the first two weeks of practice the coaches had determined that I would be a tight end, not a linebacker. I had steadily moved up the depth chart, from fourth to third string. On the last day of two-a-days, I went head to head with the first-string tight end and got the best of him. As a freshman, I ended up winning the starting tight end job on the freshman team. That gave me a lot of confidence.

Ronnie Mankin was my freshman coach. He was a very aggressive man and a great motivator who had us in top condition. The freshman team would scrimmage against the varsity team two or three times a week, and we would always hold our own. That was a credit to Maknin's commitment to making us better, and his willingness to praise us when we did well. I did my best to make him proud, as did the entire team. That year, we won all four of our games and finished first in the conference.

———

My best friend at West Texas, Ed Alford, was from Harrisburg, Pennsylvania. He was a teammate who at 6-foot-2 and 260 pounds played offensive tackle, and we were both physical education majors. Ed was a real happy-go-lucky guy, never in a bad mood, and there wasn't an ounce of prejudice in his body. We lived right next to each other in the athletic dorm and ended up being roommates my junior year.

Ed belonged to a fraternity, Lambda Chi Alpha, and he occasionally took me to the frat house to relax and play pool or other games. There was always beer and girls around, so it was a great way to socialize and not spend any money. Eventually, I joined up, and absolutely loved every minute I spent with my new frat brothers.

Socially, I was starting to loosen up. I was meeting more and more people outside of football. Yet with all the changes I was going through, I remained dedicated to my priorities: school was number one, football number two, and my social life number three.

Staying focused wasn't easy to do because things

weren't going well for Mom back in Mission. My parents divorced during my college sophomore year. The split happened during my finals, but I didn't find out until I went to visit my sister and met my mom there. When I arrived, my mother explained what had happened. But it was no surprise to me. I guess my father could have walked out much earlier, but he didn't. After the divorce, he talked with my brother and me and asked us to forgive him. He simply said that he didn't love our mom anymore. He was living with a lady whom he ended up marrying later.

Now that I'm a parent, I can see how difficult it is raising a family. I feel grateful for the time that my dad remained with our family, even if that time was less than ideal. I grew up believing that he loved all of us. Now I look back and think about how cramped we were in our little house. I can see why he felt the need to go out. But today I can't understand how a father would not want to be with his family on Christmas Eve or for his children's birthdays.

I lost contact with my dad in 1973 and didn't get back in touch with him until 1998. I took all three of my boys to meet him. We had a nice visit and it was important that my boys saw their grandfather. Unfortunately, he died shortly thereafter in a car accident.

The divorce was heartbreaking for me, as I felt more alone than ever living in north Texas. My senior year, I experienced more heartbreak. I had been dating a white girl, Sandy, for close to a year. She was a cheerleader and I was crazy about her. Her parents were wealthy and lived 15 miles from Canyon, in Happy, Texas. Her father was a football supporter and he invited me over to have

Thanksgiving dinner at his house. We had a game that Saturday, and I couldn't go home to see my mother. So I accepted his invitation.

Sandy's parents had no idea that Sandy and I were dating. After dinner, I headed into the living room to watch the Cowboys football game with Sandy's dad. Sandy joined us, plopping down on my lap and putting her arm around me. I couldn't believe it and I didn't know what to say. I was as surprised by her boldness as her father. After I left, they had a big fight. She was not allowed to see me anymore, her father said. They were concerned about what the neighbors would think. I didn't find out about any of it until after the game that Saturday. I explained to Sandy how I would understand if she didn't want to continue our relationship. But she chose to keep going out with me. She continued having arguments with her parents until it got to where she hated going home. She even considered eloping with me. She asked me how much money I had in the bank. I told her I couldn't afford to support a wife, especially since we were both still in school.

Sandy's parents finally persuaded her to break up with me. She never told me the real reason why we broke up, but I've always felt that it was the brand new Buick Regal she showed up in one day. I was crushed and it took me a long time to get over it. She was my first true love, and I never saw or heard from her again.

———

I improved every year on the football field. I was

named second team All-Missouri Valley Conference my junior year, then first team my senior year. I made it into the record books after finishing second in receptions in a single season. Still, I had some regrets. My sophomore year we finished co-champions with Tulsa University. We all had high hopes heading into my junior year, as we were picked to win the conference. But we ended the season with a disappointing 2-9 record. We also had a losing record my senior season. Playing on back-to-back losing teams left a sour taste in my mouth and certainly didn't help my stock in the NFL draft. But I was happy for other reasons following my senior year: I had attained my degree in physical education with a minor in Spanish. My number-one priority had been an overwhelming success.

Before the NFL draft I had heard from my coaches that the Minnesota Vikings were real high on me. I thought they were going to draft me, but they didn't. After the draft was over, the Kansas City Chiefs and the Atlanta Falcons both made me what I thought were real good offers to join their training camps and try out for the team. As a tight end, I felt that the Chiefs offered a better opportunity, so I accepted their offer.

I was a little slow for my position and was told that I needed to be at least an inch taller. But I was determined to train hard and make the cut. I started my training in May to be ready for rookie camp in mid-July. I got up every morning at 7:30 and ran two miles. Then I ran pass patterns for an hour with the help of Bill Delaney, a friend of mine. I had never been so disciplined, hitting the weights five days a week. I just knew I would overcome my obstacles.

The unexpected happened to me two weeks before camp. While running one of my pass patterns, I stepped in a hole and badly injured my Achilles tendon. Our team trainer, Lynn Laird, iced my ankle for 30 minutes and wrapped it for me. Then he sent me to our team doctor in Amarillo for an X-ray. He told me that I had severely sprained my Achilles tendon. He gave me a cortisone shot in the ankle and told me to stay off it. After being on crutches for a week, I returned for another cortisone shot. I was seeing Dr. Laird every day for therapy, and my ankle was getting a little better, but had not improved enough. I saw my dream of playing professional football coming to an end. I returned for my third cortisone shot on the Saturday before I left for Kansas City. I arrived in Kansas City without having run on my tender ankle for two weeks. I was worried to death.

On the morning of my first pro workout, I had the Chiefs trainer wrap my ankle really good, almost like a cast, so I wouldn't show any signs of injury. We were timed on the 12-minute run and I ran one and three-quarter miles, a good time. But I ran into trouble on the 40-yard dash. My fastest time then was 5.0 seconds, not a good time for my position. My normal speed had been 4.8, and I had been clocked at 4.7 just days before the injury. I couldn't complain about the injury, because I would lose my opportunity to prove myself. So I kept my mouth shut and got back to work.

We put on pads in the afternoon and I was ready for action. Surprisingly, my ankle was holding up great. I was in better shape than 90 percent of the 150 players who were brought in. It didn't take me long to find out that I could play in the NFL. Kansas City's number-one draft pick that year was a tight end from Kentucky, Elmore Stephens. Two weeks into practice I was playing in front of him and behind third-year player Gary Butler, who had come in late to camp. Kansas City's offensive coordinator, Bob Snelker, took a liking to me and he was very helpful. I thought about getting timed again in the 40, but I never brought it up since I was doing so well.

I was told five minutes before our first preseason game that I was going to start. I went on to start every preseason game, playing in the first half while Butler played the third quarter and Stephens the last quarter. Things were going great. The way I saw it, I was getting groomed to be the second-team tight end.

Maybe I should have seen the writing on the wall. Butler had suffered a preseason injury, and as a result the team had made two trades for tight ends. They brought in Billy Masters, an eight-year veteran from Denver, and Walter White, a third-round pick that season from the Pittsburgh Steelers. The team was developing back-up plans.

Just prior to the start of the season I got some unexpected news. All the players were in the meeting room going reviewing game film from the previous week. One of the team trainers told me that our head coach, Paul Wiggin, wanted to see me in his office. I knew right away what it was about. Coach Wiggin told me how hard it was to come to the decision to let me go. He said I was a talented athlete and had a great attitude, but because of my slow time on the 40-yard dash, they felt uneasy and couldn't trust with my inexperience. I knew he was trying to break it to me as easy as he could. I just sat there and listened without saying a word. I began to regret not getting timed again on the 40-yard dash after my ankle had healed.

I left his office, went into the locker room, and undressed. The rest of the guys were in meetings, so I was able to shed a tear or two without anyone seeing. I slowly got dressed and went outside to watch the guys practice in Arrowhead Stadium. I watched for about half an hour. Feeling lonely, I walked to the hotel where we were staying across the freeway from the stadium, went up to my room, and called my mom to give her the news. I felt that I had let down a lot of people who were so proud of me. I was looking for sympathy, but my mother wasn't about to give me any. She was actually happy.

"Good," she said, "you can come home now. I don't have to worry about you getting hurt."

Despite my mom's concern for my physical well being, I remained determined to play football. I knew I could play in the NFL, so I went back to Canyon to meet with my tight ends coach at West Texas, Jim Campbell, who had connections in the Canadian Football League. He made a couple phone calls and got me a tryout with the British Columbia Lions. I went up to British Columbia and practiced with the club for the remainder of the season. Then, I signed a contract for the 1976 season to play tight end.

The Kansas City Chiefs contacted me at the end of the 1975 season and wanted to sign me again as a free agent, but I turned them down. I figured I would play two or three seasons in Canada before trying out for the NFL again. But things don't always work out the way you plan. The Lord had something else in mind for me. He would soon reveal a career that I had never dreamed possible.

I make no apologies for the words that follow, for they are nothing but the truth. I hope the following story will inform, inspire, and remind everyone to follow his or her dreams.

Arriba!

1

BREAKING INTO
THE BUSINESS

MY INTRODUCTION

I never wanted to be a professional wrestler, but the business came to me. My friend, Tully Blanchard, was the quarterback on the West Texas State football team, and during my junior year in 1974, Tully started talking to me about becoming a wrestler. His father, Joe Blanchard, was the promoter of the Southern territory in Texas. Tully thought because I was tall and good looking that I could find more success in wrestling than in football. He concluded that I could become a hero for Mexican fans.

I had no interest in a professional wrestling career at the time, because I still had my sights set on playing in the NFL. But I didn't forget his suggestion. A few years after our initial conversation I was cut by the Kansas City Chiefs. I began to rethink the wrestling opportunity. In a conversation with Joe Blanchard, he told me I could be making $80,000 a year in no time and that I would become an idol for my Mexican peers. I still resisted, however, telling Joe that I wanted to play one more season in British Columbia and then possibly start training to be a wrestler after the 1976 football season. Since Tully would be graduating from West Texas at that time and starting his wrestling career, it made sense.

Joe knew that I didn't know much about wrestling, but he assured me that since I was a good athlete, I could pick up the moves fast. The business end of the deal sounded almost too good to be true: $80,000 a year? That sounded fine by me.

PUSHED TO MY LIMIT

Following the '76 season I went ahead with wrestling, trusting my future to Joe. He started me as a ref for matches in Texas, where I did some training as well. My stint as a ref was a way to teach me the business and to also make a little money. I spent about three weeks in Texas and then went to Tampa, Florida, with Tully, who was already wrestling full-time. In Tampa, my serious training as a wrestler began.

A typical training session began with reps of free squats and push ups mixed with long-distance running. Then, after my tongue was hanging out, I had to climb into the ring and wrestle one of the pros. The head trainer, a man in his fifties named Hiro Matsuda, would put me into submission holds. He was in great physical condition and could really ratchet up the pain. But I wasn't allowed to give up. It was all a game to him.

They were trying to stretch me, as they called it. "Stretching" was a way of weeding out those who were nondeserving of the chance to become a professional wrestler and to learn the ins and outs of the business. One had to earn the right to be smartened up. Though I was getting stretched, I was not about to become a quitter.

Matsuda and a second trainer, Bob Orton, Sr., taught me the basics, starting from scratch. The training was tough and very physical and often left my body black and blue. I never imagined it would be so tough. After those first couple training sessions, I wondered if I had made the right decision after all.

FAKE? NOT!

Professional wrestling has a reputation of being fake. All I have to say to that is you cannot fake gravity. The storylines are prepared and the winner is determined, but the wrestling is genuine. Because of this, only a select few are tough enough to make it in the business.

Many of the guys I initially trained with had no business even trying out. But they wanted to become professional wrestlers, to live out a dream. Matsuda and Orton did not take it easy on anyone. They made it tough, so that the only way you would want to come back for your next workout was if you were serious enough, and good enough, to be a pro. To be given their seal of approval, you had to pay the price.

Once I was in the ring, I realized how lethal some of the guys in the business could be. Wrestlers like King Haku and Mike Graham could easily snap a guy in half. The fact that they didn't proves they were pros. What fans never hear about is what happens in the dressing room, where action from the ring spills over and the fights become all too real. In some cases, fights will carry over from the ring to the dressing room or hotel room, or to a bar later that night. Once you leave the ring, the rules change. There is no referee and no one to ring the bell.

MEETING THE GIANT

I first met Andre "The Giant" Roussimoff in 1976 when he was 30 years old. I was refereeing his match in San Antonio right before Christmas. I remember being scared to death to blow it. He was the biggest man I had ever seen, standing 7-foot-4. His hands were huge; his pinky was a size 15. His shoe size was 22, and he weighed around 500 pounds. His large size was due to the excess secretion of pituitary growth hormone, a condition known as acromegaly.

I was lucky to meet André the Giant early in my wrestling career. We became good friends and spent a lot of time together away from the ring.

If Andre liked you, you knew it; and if he didn't like you, you also knew it. He had little privacy in his life, which I'm sure bothered him. Due to his size, he was an easy target for mean-spirited people who wanted to make fun of him. Many did so loudly and plainly, so that he could hear their remarks. For years he just took the insults. But eventually he turned mean to anyone who bothered him.

As the saying goes, he was a gentle giant to me. He took a liking to me right away, and was friendly, extending me offers to have drinks with him after matches. Wrestling was his whole life. He also loved to play cribbage, a popular game with the wrestlers, and I would play with him every night in the dressing room or at the hotel during our vast periods of down time. We played so much cribbage that I sometimes didn't have time to properly stretch. I went straight from the cribbage game to the ring.

MY FELLOW ALUMNI

Terry Funk was the NWA World Heavyweight Champion in 1977 when I broke into wrestling. It was in early 1977 when he came to Tampa to defend his title against Dusty Rhodes. Terry, who was playing a bad guy at that point in his career, sent for me to visit him in his dressing room.

We already knew each other because Terry, who also attended West Texas State, had watched me play football. I had also spoken to him during some of our football practices, well before I had become interested in wrestling. With our shared background serving to break the ice, I spoke to Terry about my first few weeks as a wrestler, and he encouraged me to stick with it. Tully planted the seed in me to become a wrestler, but Terry is the one who really encouraged it to grow. That day he became my mentor, assuring me that I would become a success.

I walked into the dressing room and Terry gave me a big hug. "How are you doing my boy! Have a seat and talk to me," he said, doing his best impersonation of promoter Jim Barnett, who owned Georgia Championship Wrestling. He grabbed his back as if he was in pain and added, "I've got to sit down."

He asked me how I was enjoying the business so far. I told him I loved wrestling, but wasn't sure if I could afford to stay involved much longer. At that point, I was a long way from that $80,000 figure that Joe Blanchard had quoted. Terry's cheerful expression faded and he said, "What do you mean?" I said, "Well, I'm learning a lot from Hiro, but I haven't made any money yet. I was told that after two weeks I would start getting matches and making some money. Well, it's been two months and I haven't earned a single penny. I haven't even had a match yet. I guess they don't think I'm ready. So I'm planning to go home soon and prepare for the football season. I'm going to return to Canada to play for the British Columbia Lions."

I continued, "Terry, I love the business, and I want to give it a shot again next year after the season is over in Canada. I just can't afford to pay the rent with no income."

"Wait a minute," he told me. "Don't do anything until

I talk to Eddie tonight, okay?"

Eddie Graham was the owner and promoter of Florida Championship Wrestling. If I got a vote of confidence from Terry, Eddie could get me a booking.

I told Terry that sounded fair and thanked him. The next morning I had a call from the secretary in the wrestling office. I had my first match scheduled that Saturday in Tampa.

MY FIRST MATCH

My first match was scheduled for March 8, 1977, in Tampa. I was pitted against a 300-pound wrestler by the name of Mike Hammer. I'll never forget the nervous tension beating me down before the match even began. I figured I could outlast the overweight wrestler. That was a big mistake.

Seven minutes into the match, Hammer laid into me, crashing his big forearm into my head. Immediately things turned around. He started putting the boots to my back as I lay on the canvas. I knew he meant business; if he was holding back at all, he had me fooled. He grabbed me by my hair to get me back on my feet, then slammed me to the canvas and came down on top of me.

I had practiced breaking a fall, but I hadn't practiced it with a 300-pound man coming down on me. He knocked the wind out of me. All of a sudden, for the first time, I heard the crowd getting into the match and rallying behind me. Although I was exhausted, I stood up, ran to the ropes, and flew at him with a cross-body. He caught me in the air and gave me a back-breaker. At that point I thought I was done. He dropped me and covered me for a pin. I raised my shoulder just in time to the roaring delight of the crowd. I was only moving on instinct by then. Hammer quickly turned to complain to the referee because he thought he had beaten me. Then he focused on me again. As he went to body-slam me, I hooked his right leg and cradled him in a small package, pinning him to the canvas. As the referee went down to count his shoulders down, the bell rang. Time had expired and the match was ruled a draw.

I was disappointed, but glad that the match had come to an end. I was dead tired and unsure if I could make it back to the dressing room on my own. The fans were still cheering me on, but I was too tired to show them any gratitude. I collapsed on the floor as soon as I made it through the doors of the dressing room.

I was congratulated by the other wrestlers for my efforts, for which I made the paltry sum of $40. That was a far cry from $1,400 I was earning a week playing football in 1976. I finally left the dressing room after all the matches were over; a few fans were waiting for wrestlers to show up and asked for my autograph. That was a first for me, and what a good feeling it was to know that I had won a few fans' support.

Although I was sore all over for days, I resumed training the next day. I knew that I had a lot more to learn. My rise to stardom clearly wasn't going to happen overnight.

DAY IN, DAY OUT

When I decided to become a wrestler, I had no idea about a wrestler's lifestyle. I figured that wrestling was like football and I would only have to wrestle in a match once a week. Little did I know that wrestlers had to wrestle a match every single night of the week. On the Florida circuit, a wrestler would have a match on Mondays in West Palm Beach and on Tuesday night make an appearance in Tampa. On Wednesday, the wrestler did a morning TV taping in Tampa and then traveled for a match that night in Miami. On Thursday it was on to Orlando, and on Friday he'd be wrestling in Sarasota. Saturdays were usually spent wrestling in Savannah, and then on Sunday the show location varied. In my short stay in Florida, I traveled mostly by car and there were usually four of us in a vehicle. I rode mainly with Angelo Poffo, a former wrestler who was promoting, in his nice Mercedes and paid him 30 cents per mile. Poffo, of course, is also the father of Randy Savage and Lanny Poffo.

A WHITE LIE

Good things started to happen to me. One night I was hanging out at the Imperial Bar in Tampa, where almost all of the wrestlers hung out after matches on Tuesday nights. Tom Renesto, who was the match-maker in Florida, came up to me and whispered, "Can I see you outside for a second?" I replied, "Sure," and we both walked outside and sat in his car.

"How'd you like to get the break of your life?" Tom asked me.

"Sure I would!" I replied. I had just a handful of matches under my belt, so the news came as a total surprise.

Tom continued, "Jim Barnett saw you on television and he loves you. You'll be making $1,500 a week and you can start on April 1."

Deep down I questioned the truth of the offer, but I decided I had no other choice but to accept. I arrived in Atlanta shortly thereafter and spoke with Jim Barnett in person. Barnett's Georgia Championship Wrestling promotion later morphed into World Championship Wrestling. We had a nice conversation, which raised my hopes about the legitimacy of Renesto's offer. As our talk came to an end, Barnett offered me a guaranteed contract—for $350 a week. I was shocked and disappointed that the rate of pay was so far off from what Renesto had stated. I couldn't pass up such an opportunity, so I decided on the spot to shake on the offer in the hopes that I could quickly work up to the $1,500 per week Renesto had promised me. I also realized later that his lie was a lesson that would help me prepare for others like him in our business. And there were plenty.

The wrestling matchmakers in Atlanta at the time were a pair of former wrestlers, Ole and Gene Anderson, who were portrayed in the ring as brothers but in truth were not. They weren't that crazy about me. I thought Ole, in particular, did not like me because of my inexperience. But it turned out that Ole was just a self-centered, obnoxious individual whose power had gone to his head. He and Gene had completely different personalities, but they both enjoyed playing stupid games with a wrestler's life and money and abusing their power.

It didn't take me long to realize there was more to the wrestling business than I'd expected. I was learning, though, and I was willing to do whatever it took to learn more. So, I put up with the many Mexican jokes and racist remarks from Ole because I had to. He enjoyed insulting everyone and often called me a "fucking Mexican." But in due time, I let him know that he would have to respect me if he wanted me to respect him.

I spent a total of ten months in Atlanta. The Atlanta territory covered the whole state of Georgia. It was a small territory and so a wrestler could only stay there for so long until he had to move on to gain more experience.

A NEW TERRITORY

After ten months, Ole finally booked me a match in Charlotte, North Carolina. George Scott was the matchmaker there. The Crockett brothers—Jim, David, and Jackie—were the promoters who owned the Charlotte territory, and George Scott ran a tight ship for them. Wrestlers had to be at the building one hour before starting time. Everyone dressed nicely, and in most cases behaved like pros. One of George's rules intended to keep up with appearances was that good guys could not travel with bad guys.

We spent more time on the road, wrestling in cities like

Raleigh, North Carolina; Richmond, Virginia; and Columbia, South Carolina. In a given week, we typically drove between 2,000 and 3,500 miles. The middle card guys like me, Randy Savage, and Tiger Conway Jr. worked 330 days out of the year. The top guys didn't have it any easier: Ric Flair, Wahoo McDaniel, and Ricky Steamboat were lucky to get more than a week off a year.

While wrestling in Charlotte, I began to polish my raw skills. Since doing interviews was very important to a wrestler's success, I practiced my interviews and speaking techniques in front of a mirror. I also used to practice with the boys—Don Kernodle, Tony Atlas, and Brian St. James— in the car as we drove from town to town. Using a beer bottle as the microphone, one of us would pretend to be both the interviewer and interviewee. It sounds crazy, but this unorthodox approach significantly helped all of us improve with our interviews.

During this point in my career, Paul Jones taught me how to properly throw a punch. There is an art to throwing a believable punch, and like any art it takes lots of practice. Paul had me tie a Styrofoam cup to a string and attach the string to the ceiling. For months I practiced throwing punches, trying to get as close to the cup as I could without making it move. After a while, I mastered it. Some wrestlers stiffened when throwing a punch and their punches don't come close to connecting, so they look unconvincing. My good friend Greg Valentine should have listened to Paul Jones and practiced with that Styrofoam cup, because he had a very stiff punch.

PINCHING PENNIES

My income went up with the move. I went from making $18,000 in 1977, to making $33,000 in 1978. That was a lot of money for a single guy who had few bills to pay. With the extra income, I was able to help my mom buy some land in Texas. The old-timers like Paul Jones and Johnny Weaver cautioned me to save my money, and I listened to them. I wasn't making the big bucks yet, but I was putting money away as much as I could.

It was sad, and a little frightening, to see some of the oldtimers toward the end of their careers failing to make ends meet. They had not properly planned. Wrestling had no unions to speak of, so wrestlers were totally on their own. With no retirement plan and no health insurance, wrestlers had to be smart with their money. Some of the guys—like Wahoo McDaniel and Ric Flair—spent their money as fast as they could make it. I paid attention to the horror stories of guys who were raking it in—some of them earning over $100,00 a year—and still had to borrow money to pay their taxes. I didn't want to end up like them.

BACK-STABBERS, CLIQUES, AND STOOGES

I spent one year in the Charlotte territory and learned a lot from guys like Paul Jones, Abe Jacobs, and Johnny Weaver. For most of that year, I was attached to one of their hips, constantly picking their brains. I was slowly learning all the tricks.

I learned that the wrestling business was all about moving up that evening's bill of wrestlers, otherwise known as "the card". The closer I got to the headlining match, the more money I earned. Wrestlers would do whatever it took to climb the ladder or keep someone else from climbing it. So I also learned plenty about back-stabbing. It wasn't unusual for the guy sitting at the top of the card to tell the promoter that he simply wouldn't wrestle a certain individual. Yet in the dressing room, he behaved like he was best friends with that same guy. The promoter, of course, would listen to his star, and the poor guy who was being singled out would never get the opportunity to make a big payday.

The cliques were a different thing. There were two or three cliques in the Charlotte territory. Usually they formed based upon lifestyle choices. Wrestlers who drank or smoked marijuana and did other drugs usually stuck together. The top stars typically formed a clique, too. The newcomers were often left to themselves, until they were able to mingle into one of the established cliques.

The other important element of wrestling that I became familiar with during this year was the "stooges," who were always around, ready to report anything they could to the promoters if it earned them a few points. Stooges were usually the referees, although once in a while a wrestler would break rank if he was told it was a matter of keeping his job. Promoters always wanted to keep tabs on what was going on after the matches, what was being said and done away from the ring. Stooges kept the promoter in the loop.

RICHARD BLOOD

At this early stage, I wasn't wrestling under my real name, Merced Solis, nor was I wrestling under the name Tito Santana. My stage name in Atlanta and Charlotte was Richard Blood, a name that was given to me by Barnett. Oddly enough, Richard Blood was Ricky Steamboat's real name. When I first arrived in Atlanta, Ricky had just left Atlanta for Charlotte. Barnett flew to Charlotte himself to meet with Ricky to get permission for the use of his given name. I guess Barnett realized he could have had a star in Atlanta had he known how to promote him. I was his shot at a makeup. I'm not sure what Ricky thought of having another wrestler on his heels, using his own name!

WOMEN!

The longer I stayed in the business, the more I thanked Terry Funk as I began to love my job. I grew to have a passion for the profession. And I have to admit, part of that passion was fueled by all the partying I did with plenty of women. Although I was still socially shy, I no longer had to worry about not having a date when I wanted to head out for a night on the town. So many women flocked to the wrestlers in the Florida, Atlanta, and Charlotte territories. It was unreal.

Promoters were very conscious of having a large number of women at the shows. Their thinking was simple: If one woman showed up and a wrestler flirted with her, pretty soon that one woman would return to a future show and bring her friends. It made good business sense because it put asses in the seats. And the ladies came in droves.

The slang for women who chased wrestlers was "Arena Rats." I saw lots of these attractive "rats," many of who chased even the unsightly wrestlers like the scary, hairy Ox Baker. Although Ox was a great guy, he was quite unattractive. So, I figured that if Ox could get a hot woman, then the world would be my oyster.

SENT TO JAPAN

Wrestling had always been big in Japan. American wrestlers who went overseas usually made good money, so most wrestlers looked forward to being booked in Japan for a few weeks.

When a guy was in between territorial moves, he could get a ticket to Japan. After I left Charlotte, I was sent to Giant Baba's promotion in Japan just after Christmas for a five-week stay that would earn me one thousand dollars per week. That was more money than I had made in the business up to that point.

HEADING HOME AS A STAR

After returning from my tour of Japan, I picked up work in the Amarillo territory in Texas, my home state. For the first time in my career, I would be at the top of the card. Black Jack Mulligan, who I befriended in Charlotte, and Dick Murdoch were the promoters. Both men had been main event wrestlers. They made good money as wrestlers in the Charlotte Territory and decided to invest. They purchased the promotion in northwest Texas from Terry Funk and Dory Funk, Jr., and began to promote as well as wrestle.

Blackjack Mulligan sincerely wanted to give me my break. The promotion's headquarters in Amarillo was just 17 miles from Canyon, where I had played football in college. Since my real name carried with it some celebrity in the area, I went back to using my real name, Merced Solis. Blackjack was banking on my name putting fans in the seats.

I also took on a new gimmick: I would be a traditional Mexican. For my new look, I got a big sombrero and wore a matching *serape*, a brightly colored wool shawl that wraps around the shoulders. The gamble worked out well for Blackjack and me. The fans loved it, and my autograph was in demand.

Blackjack was a big man, 6-foot-6 and around 300 pounds. He had long dark hair and a thick mustache and was rugged looking, like a cowboy. Dick Murdoch was also a cowboy-type, with a big belly and a few missing teeth. Like Blackjack, Murdoch was a fan favorite who enjoyed the attention. Unlike Blackjack, Murdoch never had a positive thing to say to me, and his remarks to me were often racist. I think he saw me as a real threat to take his spot and steal his fame.

The day of my first television appearance Murdoch made sure that I didn't come out looking better than him. As promoter, he booked me against Stan Lane and the match ended in a draw. I was very upset, because a draw in

TV wasn't going to help me get the big push I wanted. A couple days later, I spoke to Blackjack about my frustrations. He wasn't at the taping, and I felt he may be sympathetic toward me. After I finished complaining, he was clearly mad.

"You were supposed to get a big win on TV so you could get your push," he told me.

Murdoch was the type who would smile to your face, but would stab you in the back the next instance. He was too ignorant to see that I would be helping his new promotion by drawing Mexican fans and young kids to the matches. I had two years of wrestling behind me, and had been wrestling a minimum of 25 matches per month against some pretty good competition. I was not going to be denied my break.

ME AND THE MILLION DOLLAR MAN

I began wrestling alongside Ted DiBiase, another one of my former teammates at West Texas State, during my stay in Amarillo. This was before he took on the character, "The Million Dollar Man," that earned him fame in the WWF. DiBiase and I became better friends through wrestling than we had been while on the gridiron. He shared a lot of his knowledge with me and helped me improve my technique. He had been wrestling about one and a half years longer than I had, and his experience helped me improve in the ring. Ted was impressed by our style—we were both quick

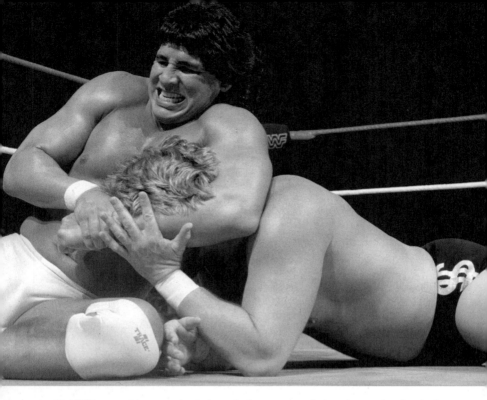

Ted DiBiase and I go way back. Long before we wrestled against each other in the WWF, we made a run at the Texas Tag Team championship.

and fearless—and the way we worked together, so he suggested to Blackjack and Murdoch that we team up and go after the Texas tag team title. I felt honored that he made the offer, as I knew that such a move would only help me make it.

The promoters agreed to the pairing, and together we started winning matches and working our way to becoming top tag team championship contenders. In early 1979, we got our shot and became Texas Tag Team Champions. Crowds were really responding to us. I had become great at playing off the crowd, bringing the fans' emotions right in the ring with me. They would tell me what they expected out of me, and I wanted them to play that role and be a big part of my success. I gave them 100-percent effort each match, knowing that they would be there for me.

Our time as champions was brief, however. After winning the tag-team belts, DiBiase and I were told we had to lose the title just one week later. Since Ted and I were moving up the ladder and drawing a large fan base, I believe Murdoch purposefully squashed our rapid success. Ted didn't take the news well; he opted to leave for New York to join the World Wrestling Federation. I stayed around Texas a while longer. At the time I had nowhere else to go.

But help was on the way. Andre the Giant had wrestled for a week in the Amarillo territory. During this time, we became even closer friends. He knew that I was miserable in the territory and that Murdoch was sabotaging my career. With great empathy, Andre sent Vince McMahon Sr., a tape of one of my matches in the hopes that I, too, could land a spot in New York.

2

MAKING A NAME FOR MYSELF

MEETING VINCE SR.

Thanks to the help of André the Giant and promoter Mario Savoldi, I was granted a shot at the WWF. My starting date was set for the middle of June 1979. Mario told me that Vince McMahon Sr., the most respectable promoter in the business, wanted me to come to New York at the same time Ted DiBiase was scheduled to arrive. I had never dreamed of getting there so soon.

McMahon was a very classy man who was in his early sixties when I first met him. He was tall, fit, and well groomed, his hair a pleasant shade of gray. McMahon was a very sharp dresser with a large wardrobe of stylish suits. He had taken over the business from his grandfather, who had started out as a boxing promoter years ago. McMahon ran the WWF from one of his two homes: he spent the winters in Florida and lived on Cape Cod during the other months. He had several road agents who would report dollars and cents to him every night, and also fill him in on how the show had gone.

ADJUSTING TO LIFE AT THE TOP

The wrestlers stayed busy in the WWF. In addition to regular matches for live audiences, we would have to participate in televised performances every three weeks. We would arrive for TV tapings usually around 2:00 p.m., and would finish up after midnight. When McMahon wasn't being tied up on the business side of things, he did make himself available to the wrestlers. That gave us an opportunity to air any complaints in private. McMahon had a way of making a wrestler feel good about himself. Of course, the more important the wrestler was, the longer Vince talked to him.

The wrestling business is like no other. We have no set pay scale, no union to protect us, and no benefits whatsoever. We were paid weekly, and could draw one or two hundred dollars each night that we wrestled. But we had little way of forecasting our pay, because we got paid whatever the company thought we were worth. That could change from one week to the next, so there was little stability. We were considered self-employed, yet we could only wrestle for the company to which we were bound by a verbal agreement. That prevented us from wrestling in multiple territories at once, and to a degree limited our exposure.

I remember wrestling in Philadelphia against the Iron Sheik in a semifinal of the main event. I was paid $1,200 for the match. The next month, I went back to Philadelphia and again wrestled the Iron Sheik, this time in the main event. I was higher up on the card and the attendance increased, but my pay went down to $750. I very politely brought it to their attention, and they immediately agreed and gave me another $750. In a few cases, I had to fight for my money. I didn't have an agent and I had to handle everything myself.

I didn't come into the WWF with any promises, but I didn't need any. I just focused on working hard and being dependable. I'll never forget my first time I wrestled at Madison Square Garden. The attendance that night was 22,000, and I wrestled against Johnny Rodz. It was easily the biggest night of my young career, and I made the most of it. Vince Sr. gave me a chance, and I didn't let him down. I was as nervous as could be, but I managed to get by without messing up the match.

In 1979, I introduced a different type of wrestling to the company: I took things to the air. My roots in the Southern territories provided me with exceptional training and plenty of experience wrestling against some of the best in the business. I also learned to use skill, finesse, and creativity to my advantage. But the WWF was very different from the South. The WWF had great big, powerful guys.

The fans were used to these hulking wrestlers, not wrestlers who preferred flying maneuvers to brute force.

When I started, I threw drop kicks, did flying head scissors and arm drags, and a few other aerial moves. I had a lot of energy, and my repertoire of moves was quite different from the style of the big guys I was wrestling against. My different style helped me catch the fan's interest. Almost immediately, I had a supportive fan base.

LEARNING A THING OR TWO

The popular Bruno Sammartino was the WWF World Champion at this time. With his name atop a card, shows sold out at Madison Square Garden and the Boston Garden time after time. He wrestled for over 20 years, and held the title of World Champion for 13 years. But he was never a superstar nationally or internationally like Hulk Hogan, because he only wrestled in the eastern part of the country. Still, Bruno was clearly the best wrestler of his era, much like Hogan.

Bruno was a rugged, powerful wrestler. Toward the later part of his career, we tagged together and enjoyed good chemistry in the ring. He was very proud of himself and the business, and he was a great role model for younger wrestlers like me.

My aerial moves earned me the respect of my peers and my boss.
Photo courtesy of Tito Santana

I learned all my moves by watching other wrestlers. If I liked a move, I would try it out that night. I modeled my matches after a lot of different wrestlers, too, but no one in particular. I incorporated what I had learned into my own distinct style, and provided a fresh face for the WWF. It seemed like by the time most wrestlers got the call to go to New York, they were already veteran, polished wrestlers. I had only been in the business for two and a half years, so I had some work to do before I would be main-event material. I was just glad to be in New York and part of the best wrestling territory in the world.

GAINING VINCE'S RESPECT

McMahon liked my aerial moves and my style in the ring. He took an interest in me and I began my move up the ranks from "curtain jerker" to wrestling in the middle of the card. My hard work was paying off. After just two months in the WWF, McMahon presented me with a huge trophy on TV and called me "Rookie of the Year." The trophy presentation was shown throughout the WWF viewing audience, which at that time included all of New York, New Jersey, Connecticut, Rhode Island, Massachusetts, and Pennsylvania. We had a potential viewing audience of 80 to 100 million people. Because of my rising stardom, it seemed like people recognized me wherever I went.

Vince knew exactly how to bring a wrestler along. His sense of timing and pace was exceptional. Four months into my WWF career he gave me a title push, teaming me with Polish wrestler Ivan Putski, who went by the nickname the "Polish Power." After a while, we won the WWF Tag Team Championship belts.

Thanks to that push, I was now making more money than I had ever made in my life.

TINO OR TITO?

When I came into the WWF, I became Tito Santana. I was the one who picked my new wrestling name; at least the last name. When I first arrived in New York, McMahon asked me to come up with a catchy name. A couple of days later, at a TV taping, I mentioned to Vince that I liked the name "Santana." He wanted to know if it was a common name. I gave him a little history about the name, telling him that there was a Spaniard named Santa Anna who had switched sides and fought bravely for Mexico's independence from Spain in the early nineteenth century. Santa Anna also later led Mexican troops at the Battle of the Alamo and the Battle of San Jacinto.

About a week later at another TV taping, Vince told me my wrestling name would be Tino Santana, which I enthusiastically accepted. Few people know this, but my first match in the WWF I wrestled as "Tino" Santana. After the match was over, Vince said to me when I got back to the dressing room, "From now on you are going to wrestle as "Tito" not "Tino" Santana. I replied, "I like it. If it is good enough for you, then it is good enough for me."

VINCE McMAHON JR.

I was getting lots of TV and magazine coverage after winning the tag team title with Putski. Every match I was competing against top wrestlers and doing weekly interviews. There I was, only three years in the business and already a tag-team champion in the number-one wrestling league in the world.

It was at this time that I got to know Vince McMahon Jr. During this stage of his career, Vince was just a commentator. He was about 35 years old in 1980 when I met him. An athletic man who was well put together, Vince Jr., or "Vinnie" as we called him, was a weightlifter. During our interview sessions, he would interview wrestlers for seven or eight hours at a time, non-stop. He never complained. He was very much like his dad, a down-to-earth guy who treated everyone with a certain amount of respect. He had a way of making you feel important.

Vinnie started out like his dad, but as the WWF grew, his personality changed. When Vinnie took over for his Dad, he was no longer our friend. He was now the boss and we called him "Vince." As the company expanded, so did the salaries of some of its wrestlers. Along with that salary came more prominence. Guys like Jake Roberts and Roddy Piper were making more money than ever before, but they couldn't handle their newfound stardom. I believe many of my fellow wrestlers did not understand who was responsible for their fame. Even today, some guys don't understand that Vince made them stars. They may have been good workers, but Vince made them superstars. I began to realize this even more when I got into the production side of the business. Vince had his hand in everything, and he and he alone, decided who would be a star in the business.

3

TIME WELL SPENT IN THE AWA

HITTING THE ROAD

After a year in the WWF I had won and lost the tag-team title. Vince McMahon Sr. told me that I needed to gain some additional experience in different territories. Then, when the time was right, he would bring me back to the WWF and put me in a very good money-making position. I respected Vince and his opinion, so I agreed to the move. "Whatever you think is best for my career," I told him.

Since Vince Sr. was so respected by other promoters, he could get me into any territory. He asked me if I had a specific place in mind. I suggested the American Wrestling Alliance (AWA), run by Verne Gagne, in Minneapolis. I

33

chose the AWA because of its great reputation and lighter work schedule than the other territories. In the AWA, a wrestler could actually have a normal life.

Vince Sr. met with me again just a few weeks later and told me that I would be finishing up at the end of April 1980. He had booked me a stint in Japan, making $1,800 a week after taxes for six weeks. Upon my return, I would then have a week off before heading to the AWA. My second trip to Japan was a great experience. I was on the same tour with André the Giant, Hulk Hogan, Dusty Rhodes, Chavo Guerrero, and a few other Americans. André the Giant was a big star at that time, so sponsors would take him out every night and wine and dine him. He would always bring me along for the ride. I recall one night we went out to see a movie and the characters were drinking wine throughout. After the movie, André and I went to a restaurant for dinner. Sure enough, he ordered a bottle of wine. To my chagrin, however, this bottle cost $200. I couldn't believe it. André just laughed and said, "Drink, Boss!"

André always treated me like a younger brother. He was so good to me, and he made my time overseas so enjoyable.

BACK IN THE STATES

Upon joining the AWA, I was reunited with Dino Bravo, a good friend of mine from my days in Atlanta. An incredibly powerful Italian wrestler who had received his big push in the Montreal territory, Dino was a classy guy. He immediately took me under his wing, gave me some pointers, and trained with me at the gym. We were inseperable, and he made my transition to the AWA a simple one.

The AWA had a reputation for being an easy place to work. It didn't pay as well as other territories, but the wrestling schedule was much lighter. Wrestlers worked only 200 to 220 days a year, leaving plenty of days off. In the WWF, I was lucky if I had two days off a month. The AWA only had about 16 regular wrestlers and only one event per night. The WWF, by comparison, had 40 regular guys and ran in two different towns per night.

Verne Gagne ran things in an entirely different fashion than Vince McMahon Sr. The pair were a study in opposites: Vince was a tall, well-dressed man; Verne was short and bald. Vince never wrestled; when I met Verne, he was in his late fifties and still the AWA World Heavyweight Champion. (He held the title well into his sixties!) The two companies had a completely different attitude about the business. Vince's focus was on moving the company into the entertainment phase; all he was interested in was selling out arenas. On the other hand, Verne wanted everyone to think that the business was totally on the up and up. He did not want the good guys hanging around with the bad guys; he expected believability. I don't know why he thought that people would believe that a 60-year-old man could beat Hulk Hogan, though.

THE UNFRIENDLY SKIES

Up until then, it was necessary for me to drive to all the different cities. AWA wrestlers flew in Verne's small Cessna plane most of the time. We'd leave our house at five o'clock in the evening and be home most of the time by midnight. We did have a few close calls in the plane. One time, the pilot forgot to switch gas tanks, which left us wondering if we would have enough fuel to make it. Another time, one of the wrestlers, who was drunk, opened the rear door in flight. That raised a few heart rates. And there was at least one emergency landing at an air force base due to fog. For someone who wasn't so accustomed to flying, I did all right. I never developed a fear of flying.

GENE OKERLUND

I believe that the two years I spent in the AWA were the most valuable years in my career. The only way to get to the top is to compete against the best, and I did just that for my two years in Minnesota. One area where I improved immensely was in my interviews. I gained invaluable experience by both practicing and learning from other guys who were already great interviewees, like the Crusher,

Dino Bravo and I in the ring. He was a classy guy and a powerful wrestler who made my transition to the AWA a smooth one.

Baron Von Rashke, and Mad Dog Vachon.

Gene Okerlund, the television commentator at that time in the AWA, handled all the interviews. He was so good at his job. He could lead you along, and if you messed up he could even help get you out of a mess. Gene knew I was young and inexperienced when it came to TV interviews, so he was always there with the right questions. He later rose to national prominence as "Mean Gene" with the WWF, but he was hardly mean spirited in real life. He is simply the best. He is to wrestling what John Madden is to the NFL.

THE LOVE OF MY LIFE

I did not date much at all in my early career. I had met lots of girls who were wrestling fans, but I never remained anywhere long enough to develop a serious relationship. I had always wanted to meet someone who knew nothing about the wrestling business. One day, my prayer was answered.

I was living in Lake Hiawatha, New Jersey, when I met my wife at a local bar called The Quarry. It was the first time I had been in there in almost a year. I've never been much into bars, but that particular night I was with wrestler Steve Travis. He was staying at my apartment for the night, and after a WWF show he wanted to go get a beer. Never one to pass up a beer, I headed with him to the Quarry. We had just sat down at a table when a beautiful woman walked in. She was wearing a long, blue cotton dress. Her light brown hair was down to her waist. As I stared, she walked right by our table. I continued to stare at her beautiful, big green eyes. I think Steve could tell I was in awe. I turned to him and said, "I'm in love."

The woman and her friend sat across the dance floor from us. She didn't even acknowledge me. I told Steve, "See those two girls? I'll buy you another beer if you talk to them." Then I added a stipulation to the offer: "But the one with the long hair is mine." He said, "For a beer I'll do it." I'm glad Steve was with me, because I was too shy to talk to a woman out of the blue.

Steve went up and told them, "My friend and I are lonely," and pointed at me. "Do you mind if we join you?" Leah, my future wife, liked Steve's line, so she said yes. I was waved over by Steve and I introduced myself to both girls, but I was only interested in the woman with those stunning green eyes.

Leah was very soft-spoken with a lovely smile. Our conversation flowed with ease. She was a very good-looking girl, but I could tell that she was not hung up on herself. It was also wintertime, so I was intrigued as to why she had such a gorgeous tan. After we chatted, I found out that she was living in Hawaii and was in town visiting her parents who lived nearby.

Twenty years later, I still can't believe I'm married to such a beautiful and compassionate woman. Through both the good and bad times, she has always been by my side. To this day, I'd still buy Steve another beer. He deserves it for breaking the ice.

WRESTLING WITH THE HULKSTER

At about the same time as me, Hulk Hogan joined the AWA. Hulk had a major role in the third *Rocky* movie with Sylvester Stallone. Vince Sr. didn't want Hulk to star in the movie because it would have taken him away from wrestling and he would have also lost control of his career. Verne, on the other hand, took advantage of the situation, playing scenes of the movie on his wrestling program to promote Hogan. So when Hulk came into the AWA he was on fire.

He was supposed to be a villain in the AWA, but the fans kept cheering him on. Verne tried his best to turn the fans against Hulk by having him beat up two guys at once, but it didn't work. Eventually Verne quit trying and let the Hulk be a babyface.

From that point on, Hulk was the biggest attraction in wrestling. Starring in the *Rocky* movie had a lot to do with it. But he was also so impressive in the ring. People couldn't believe their eyes. He was solidly built and stood 6-foot-7. For his size, he was very quick. His physical attributes were only part of the reason he became so beloved. More importantly, he was exceptionally charismatic. Fans loved everything about him. So did many of his fellow wrestlers. When the arenas were full—and with Hulk on the card they always were—we all made money. I consider myself lucky to have been with Hulk for most of my career. He made my career a success.

Throughout the years, I have heard and read others knock Hulk's talent. But I honestly believe it all has to do with jealousy. The wrestling business is about who can get people to buy tickets or tune in on TV. Without reservations, I can say that nobody ever did it better than the Hulk.

SARGE

To this day, Robert Remus, better known to wrestling fans as Sgt. Slaughter, is one of my best friends. I first met Sarge in 1977 while working in the Atlanta territory. But we really got to know each other well in the AWA.

When I came into the territory, Sarge was getting a big push. Don Kernodle and I put him over in a handicapped match, which put Sarge in line to make thousands upon thousands of dollars. As a result, Sarge never forgot that match. In fact, as he was on his way out of the AWA, he personally asked Verne to book us together in a match in which he lost to help put me over.

We eventually hooked up again when wrestling in the WWF. We have been close friends ever since. Due to our friendship and passion for the wrestling business, Sarge and I opened our own promotion after both of us left the company in 1993. Our company, the American Wrestling Federation (AWF) folded after about a year. Sarge is currently a road agent with the WWE, and I hope the young talents take advantage of his expertise and knowledge of the business.

4

A COSTLY MISTAKE

ON THE MOVE AGAIN

Verne Gagne cited my own overexposure and the AWA's influx of several new babyfaces when serving me notice that it was time to move on. The move couldn't have come at a worse time for me personally. My new wife, Leah, was six months pregnant.

Verne recommended a few places and left the decision up to me. The places he recommended were Joe Blanchard's south Texas territory, and Jim Barnett's Atlanta territory. Since Joe gave me my introduction to the business, I called Tully, his son and my friend and fellow wrestler. He told me that they could guarantee me a spot, but could not offer any guaranteed money. On the other hand, Jim had given me my first steady job in the business. When I spoke with him, he promised me both a spot and guaranteed that I would make a $1,000 a week.

I was leaning toward Atlanta, but I called my mentor, Vince McMahon Sr. I wanted to check in with him and also ask for his advice and guidance. Although Vince left the decision entirely up to me, he recommended Atlanta over Texas. He said that going to Atlanta would get me a considerable amount of TV coverage, as the territory's matches were often television by Ted Turner's TBS network. And TBS was broadcasting nationwide. I listened to Vince and decided to go to Atlanta.

Jim Barnett once again treated me with a vast amount of respect. In addition to the pay, Jim gave me a day off every other week. But Ole Anderson was still the match-maker in that territory. It was known that I wasn't crazy about him, and I know he wasn't crazy about me. But I thought that we could work together. At first, Ole told me that they were going to make me a big international star because of the nationwide TBS TV coverage. Although I was skeptical, I wanted to believe him.

FROM GOOD TO BAD

It took only three months in Atlanta for me to realize that Ole had no intention of living up to his word. At that time, Ole was making his move, trying to take over the

Atlanta territory from Jim. Somehow he double-crossed Jim and took control of the company.

When I agreed to come Atlanta, Ole was only the match-maker. But now he had complete control. I had a verbal agreement with Jim that my weekly pay would be no less than $1,000. The deal included an arrangement for me to travel to Ohio every nine weeks or so. For this extra effort, Jim promised me anywhere between $1,400 and $1,800 per week. When Ole took over, he made it pretty clear that he wanted me out. He never had any plans for me to get a push, and if that wasn't clear enough he cut my pay to $850 to $900 per week when I was traveling to Ohio, and to a measly $350 to $400 per week while in Atlanta.

Ole let me know he was now in charge. He arrogantly came right out and told me that it was Jim who had wanted me there, not him. He said he didn't have a spot for me, but that I could continue to work for him if I wanted. I knew he was lying because in the same breath Ole asked me if I was interested in going to work for Bill Watts in Louisiana. With Leah due in a few weeks, I had no plans on going anywhere and told Ole as much. He replied, "Fine, but there are no guarantees."

I knew that Bill Watts was very interested in me wrestling for him. However, he and Ole were good friends, and my gut told me they had a game plan to get me to Louisiana. It almost worked. Bill and his match-maker, Ernie Ladd, had traded phone calls with me in an effort to convince me to join them in the Bayou. But they balked at my asking price of a $2,000 per week guarantee.

The main reason I didn't want to go to Louisiana was

because my good friend, Paul Orndorff, had already told me all I needed to know about Bill and the Louisiana territory. Paul had wrestled in Louisiana for Bill and told me the trips were very long and the money was not what you deserved. Basically, Paul told me, Bill Watts was in the business of taking advantage of young wrestlers. Watts' territory stretched from Houston, Texas, through all of Oklahoma down through all of Louisiana. So it was not unusual to travel 400 miles each way by car just to do a single match. Wrestlers were also expected to work seven days a week for payoffs in the pits.

I didn't want to go somewhere where I'd be gone from my family most of the time. I politely declined to sign with Bill.

A PROUD FATHER

During all these discussions with Bill Watts, my son was born on December 27, 1982. I was with my wife when she went into labor, canceling my tour to Ohio that Christmas week to be sure I was there for the birth. Ole was not happy that I stayed behind. He wanted complete control of my life. I told him simply, "My family comes first."

We spent that Christmas Eve at the hospital, but it was a false alarm. Our son, Matthew Ryan, was born two days later. He was healthy and so was my wife, and that was the only thing that mattered at the time. I was the happiest man in the world. I had a beautiful wife and a beautiful, healthy son.

SCREWED AGAIN BY OLE

When I told Bill no, I thought that was the end of it. Sadly, it wasn't. I was about to get another education on how bookers and promoters like to mess with a wrestler's life. Although I had also told Ole that I wasn't going to Louisiana, he went ahead and booked me there the first week of February 1983. He told me that I was only going for eight days, and that Bill had agreed to pay me $2,500 for the tour. I didn't have a choice if I wanted a paycheck that week. So along with Butch Reed, I headed to Louisiana for the eight-day stint. Neither one of us had any idea what to expect. The only thing we knew was that Ole was ready to get rid of both of us.

We wrestled eight nights straight, beginning in Shreveport, before traveling to Tulsa and Oklahoma City, then to Baton Rouge, Little Rock, Houston, and a few other cities. I didn't enjoy the travel, but the pay was nice. Still, I knew the only reason they were paying me well was because Ole wanted me to go work for Bill. It wasn't likely that my pay would remain that high, because Bill had already told me as much when I declined his initial offer.

When I returned to Atlanta, Ole kept me around a few more weeks but cut my pay more and more. In March, I returned to Louisiana for a five-day tour. Again, Bill paid me more money than I was making on similar trips from Georgia to Ohio. The message from the two promoters was clear: move to Louisiana, or else. Ole had cut my pay by such a staggering amount that I could no longer afford to live in Atlanta. Ole had won the game. I now had no choice but to sign with Bill. After all the misery that Ole had put me through, I was ready to move on. I was sure from speaking with Orndorff that I wasn't going to enjoy working for Bill, but at this point I was resigned to choosing the pain I didn't know over the pain I did know.

I had discussed the move with Leah, and if Bill would make me a decent offer I was ready to sign on with him. I figured that Bill would be happy to hear that I was ready to negotiate. But his response was decidedly lacking in emotion. He told me he'd talk to me about it in a few days. I could see that I had probably lost all negotiating power with Bill. That got the wheels churning in my mind again. I had to do something, and quick.

THE PHONE CALL

That Wednesday morning, I got up early and called Vince McMahon Sr. in New York. I told him how Ole had been treating me so poorly and that I couldn't take it any longer. I explained how Bill had showed an interest in me, and that I would be talking to him that Friday about making a permanent move to Louisiana. Vince told me that Bill was a good man to work for, and that it would be a good move for me. That wasn't the response I was hoping to hear. I had hoped that Vince would tell me that I had suffered enough, that it was time to pack my bags for New York to return to the fold.

The next day, I drove with Junk Yard Dog, a black

wrestler who was very popular in Louisiana, from Tulsa to Houston. It was there that Bill and I would meet, under his terms. I entered the dressing room and was taken aside by Ernie Ladd. "Tito," he told me, "tonight you'll have to make the biggest decision of your life."

I just looked at him, dumbfounded. I had no idea what he was talking about. Ernie continued, "Vince Sr. called Bill and told him that he wants you back in the WWF. He wants you to call him Saturday morning." I was the happiest man in the world. The decision would not be a difficult one.

About 30 minutes later, Bill walked into the dressing room. I acted surprised when he told me about Vince's call. Bill told me what a great talent I was and how he wanted me to work for him. He told me how he could help me with the little things that he thought that I was still lacking on the business end of things, particularly my ability at handling promotional interviews. I believed Bill really felt he could help me out, but I didn't want to hang around to find out. He asked me to take some time before making a decision, adding, "Whatever you decide, you will remain in good standing with me."

The next morning, I called Vince. When he answered and I identified myself, all I heard was silence on his end. The silence lasted for about 30 seconds, but it seemed like eternity. I started to think that maybe Vince was in on this whole thing with Ole and Bill. I had anticipated a warm response from Vince, and for him to launch into the terms of his offer; but I was greeted by silence. I couldn't take it any longer, so I spoke first and with a disappointed tone said to Vince Sr. "that the reason I had called was because I was told to do so." At that moment his response was, "Yes, Tito, it's time for you to come home." He said, "Your starting date will be May 10, 1983."

I was ecstatic! I'll never forget that day because it was also my birthday. What a present! I said to him, "Vince, that's all I needed to hear. Thank you!" I couldn't wait to hang up and give my wife the good news.

BYE BYE, OLE

When I got back to Atlanta, I gave Ole my notice. He tried to talk me into staying. I couldn't believe he had the nerve. What a scumbag! He revealed his plans to take wrestling down to South America, and told me that he wanted to make me one of his top guys. It all sounded like a load of crap. I thought, "Ole, have you no sense of decency?"

I respectfully gave him my three-week notice. When I got home, Leah and I had a small celebration and began counting the days until our move back to New York City.

5

BACK IN THE WWF

RIGHT PLACE AT THE RIGHT TIME

My first WWF TV tapings upon my return were very successful. Vince McMahon Sr. reinforced that I had made the correct move. He had a gift of making me feel great about myself. I believe that gift played a large role in why I've never heard anyone say a bad thing about the man. And it's very rare to be able to say that about a promoter.

Some of the biggest breaks for athletes—just like all people—come from being at the right place at the right time. Fortunately for me, the right time to reenter the WWF was May 10, 1983. Jimmy "Superfly" Snuka, one of the biggest stars in the WWF at that time, suddenly found himself in a world of trouble related to the accidental death of his close friend. She died from a fractured skull. Due to an ongoing investigation by authorities, and to cope with the loss, Snuka took some time off and missed a bunch of bookings. I was the lucky and unlucky one to take his place. The reason I say unlucky is because when fans pay to see someone—in this case, Snuka—that's who they want to see. I got bumped into Snuka's spot, and fans didn't hesitate to let me know that they were not pleased.

I made the best of an awkward situation, showing up to work and doing my best to ease the transition for the WWF.

SAYING GOODBYE TO SENIOR AND HELLO TO JUNIOR

I had only been in the WWF a few short months when a large meeting was called to inform us about a change in leadership. Vince Sr. announced that Vinnie would be taking over. Declining health had a lot to do with Vince Sr. handing the business over to his son. He became ill from prostate cancer shortly after the meeting.

Upon taking over the reins, Vinnie became Vince. He went from being a friend to my boss. Vince let us know that there were many changes ahead; he had big plans and predicted a major growth period for the WWF. Vince was a workaholic and had a tremendous amount of energy and enthusiasm. If anyone would be able to initiate such growth, it would be Vince.

The WWF did indeed grow, but his father never got to see it. Shortly after Vince Jr. took over the company, Vince

Sr. passed away from cancer in May 1984. Sadly, none of the wrestlers went to his funeral. We were all too busy wrestling in a business that never stopped.

When Vince Sr. passed, the world had lost a great man and a true credit to the wrestling profession.

THE COMPANY EXPANDS

Under Vince Jr., the WWF went from being just an east coast promotion to a national and even international affair. In a short period of time, the company left behind its hotel-room office in Manhattan and moved into a huge office building in Stamford, Connecticut. Suddenly, we went from traveling a little to traveling a lot. On the plus side, the wrestlers' pay also went up significantly; mine quadrupled.

In all fairness to Vince, he had a big dream that unfolded bigger than he had expected. WrestleMania I was in New York's Madison Square Garden with a capacity of 22,000 people. WrestleMania III was held at Detroit's Pontiac Silver Dome, and featured over 93,000 fans. I don't think anyone envisioned that kind of growth spurt.

WRESTLEMANIA I

In March of 1985, at the Madison Square Garden in New York City, in front of 20,000 plus people, I opened the first ever WrestleMania against a masked wrestler named The Executioner, otherwise known as Buddy Rose. I was very upset before WrestleMania because Greg Valentine and I were engaged in a great program and drawing very well on the road. I couldn't understand why Greg and I couldn't have a main-event match at the unprecedented event. At the time, George Scott was the booker. I found out later that the reason why we didn't wrestle a main-event match was because our matches were so good that they wanted the angle to hit every individual city we toured, and not expose it at a Pay-Per-View event.

Before I went out to the ring for my match, Vince said to me, "Tito, I have everything riding on this Pay-Per-View. If it doesn't work out, we are going down. If it is successful, we are off and running and nothing can stop us. I put you in the first match because I want to get the people off their butts right off the bat, and you're the one that can do it." The genuine pep talk made me feel real good.

I had a good opening match with Buddy. After about five minutes, he submitted to a figure-four leg lock, giving me the win. The crowd was going crazy, so I was happy that I had accomplished Vince's goal of energizing the audience. The early match also worked out good for my program with Valentine. During his match later in the night against Junk Yard Dog, I interrupted their match—in what we call a "run in"—after Greg had pinned JYD by rolling him up while holding the ropes for leverage. I came out and told the referee about the cheating, and the ref reversed the decision and restarted the match. Valentine refused to continue and walked out of the ring. The referee disqualified him and JYD was declared the winner. Valentine was livid and he blamed me for the loss. This added fuel to the fire for our rivalry.

The main event in the first WrestleMania was Hulk Hogan and tough-guy actor Mr. T versus Roddy Piper and Mr. Wonderful. My good friend André the Giant was also on the card in a $15,000 body slam gimmick match against Big John Studd, which André won by slamming the "unslammable" Studd. After the match, André threw real money into the crowd, which was going bananas.

A WHO'S WHO AT WRESTLEMANIA

The first WrestleMania was an unprecedented event for pro wrestling. It took the WWF national and successfully brought the sport into the mainstream. Prior to Vince's brilliant marketing strategy, wrestling was a regional sport that catered to the rough and tough crowd. But after the first WrestleMania, things changed. Vince made certain that WrestleMania would be an event to see and be seen at for famous Hollywood actors and celebrity personalities. I couldn't believe who I spotted in the crowd, from New York Yankees manager Billy Martin, to pop singer Cyndi Lauper, to the greatest heavyweight boxer of all time, Muhammad Ali.

I also met a pair of flamboyant people that night that I will never forget, iconic artist Andy Warhol and legendary entertainer Liberace. It turned out that Warhol wasn't just a professional wrestling fan, but a fan of *me*. He made his way to the locker room in the hopes of meeting me. We chatted for a while and I was impressed with his personality and character. I gave him my autograph and we had some pictures taken with each other. Liberace was there with the Rockettes. He put on a great performance right in the middle of the wrestling ring. Afterward, I had a chance to visit with him in the locker room for about ten minutes. He was very polite and quite a small person. He told me that he respected what the wrestlers were doing and how hard they worked—a compliment that meant a lot to me.

THE ANIMATED TITO

Building on the success of the first WrestleMania, Vince produced a Saturday-morning cartoon series featuring most of the big-time WWF wrestlers, including me. The show was titled after Hogan, *Hulk Hogan's Rock 'n' Wrestling*, and also featured Rowdy Roddy Piper, Superfly Snuka, the Iron Sheik, Nikolai Volkoff, the Fabulous Moolah, Junkyard Dog, André the Giant, Big John Studd, Wendi Richter, Captain Lou Albano, and Mr. Fuji, among others.

I made some money off the cartoon, which ran for nearly two years beginning in September 1985, but not very much. I didn't do the voiceover for my character. From what I understand, Vince didn't want the wrestlers' real voices for the cartoon, so he hired actors to do our voices. But on occasion I would go to Los Angeles and tape some promotional commercials for the cartoon.

My kids got to see me as a cartoon character, which

made them happy. I taped all the episodes and still have them in storage for the future grandchildren to enjoy.

INTERCONTINENTAL CHAMPION

I won the Intercontinental belt the first time in 1984 by defeating the muscle-bound Don "The Rock" Muraco at the Boston Garden. Too bad they never got it all on film. That night, Hulk Hogan had wrestled in an earlier match, and Don and I went on last. I was already ticked off because Vince and all the WWF big shots left the arena before my match was over so they could beat the crowd. They would have never treated Hogan with that lack of respect. After the match, I found out that the filming crew just happened to run out of film, so the move that I used to beat Muraco that night was never seen by anyone other than the fans in attendance.

My hurt feelings were patched up a bit when I found out just how much money I was scheduled to make that year. I had been making around $60,000 a year during my first couple years in the league. I was trying to purchase my first house in Flanders, New Jersey, for $119,000. I thought I was going to have a hard time scrounging up the money to afford the home, but when I called the WWF office and asked them if they could help me out a little, they told me that my projected income for 1984 would be $176,000! You can imagine the look of shock on my face. Needless to say, we got the house.

THE DAILY GRIND

My wrestling schedule didn't leave much time for beauty rest. I averaged three days off every 90 days, and my routine became exceedingly precise. I typically got up at 5:30 a.m., showered, and headed to the airport to catch the first flight out to whatever city I was booked in that day. I was always worried about being late for an event, so I made certain to be at the airport early to catch the first plane. In my 12 years of working with the WWF, I only missed two flights, and in both instances it was due to a forgotten wake-up call.

After checking in at the airport, I would eat breakfast. As I waited at the gate, I would call Leah from a pay phone. It's too bad cell phones weren't around back then. The airplane flight gave me a chance for a nap, and I always took advantage of the opportunity. The sky was my favorite place to catch up on some quality sleep.

Upon landing, I would immediately head to the rental car desk. I had to make all my own car and hotel reservations, as well as pay for everything. I favored larger vehicles, like a Lincoln Continental, because I often had to share the car with other wrestlers. We would split the costs and share driving duties.

From the airport, I would head straight to the hotel, check in, eat a large lunch, then go straight to the local gym for an hour-and-a-half-long workout. Gold's Gym was my preference, but any gym close to the hotel would work.

It was good to have the Intercontinental belt around my waist.

Lifting weights and staying in shape was very important to me, so I worked out four to five times a week regardless of my travel schedule. I learned how to put together an efficient travel workout from Tony Atlas and Paul Orndorff. I usually did about 20 minutes of cardio, then I would switch to weights. One day I would work on my chest, triceps, and shoulders; the next I would focus on my back and biceps; and on the third day I would work out my legs. If I had some extra time, I would always do some additional cardio exercise, because it was key to my endurance in the ring.

After my workout, I would head back to the hotel, clean up, then head out with the boys to grab a light snack and chew the fat. Afterwards, I would take a break, usually between an hour and two hours. During that time, I'd watch TV or take a nap, and be sure to call Leah again. Then it was off to the arena.

At the venue I would first check in with the road agents, usually former wrestlers like Chief Jay Strongbow, Rene Goulet, and Pat Patterson. They would post the schedule and address that event's wrestlers with any concerns. While I waited for the night's events to get underway, I would play cribbage with André, stretch, and get dressed for my match. After my turn in the ring, I would shower and wait for the other wrestlers I had traveled to the venue with to finish up. Then we would leave the venue together, often around 11:30 p.m., and head back to the hotel.

Back in my room, I'd check in with my wife for the third time, then head to the hotel lounge or restaurant for a late dinner and drinks with the boys. I usually ended up back in my room by 1 a.m. to catch a few hours of sleep before my 5:30 wake-up call.

LOSING THE TITLE

By October of 1985, I had been champion for eight months. I was gaining momentum, holding my own in all my title defenses and building a really solid fan base. I had injured my knee eight days earlier in Los Angeles in a match against Mr. Wonderful, Paul Orndorff. Paul was one of my close friends in the business and he ribbed me often, busting my chops because I always flossed my teeth in the locker room, or playing tricks on me by putting Tabasco sauce and salt in my coffee. Paul had a great look and was one of the best heels ever. The way he could work the crowd was unequaled by his peers. But, he was also an atom bomb waiting to explode. If he wasn't happy with one of his payoffs, he was capable of just quitting. He didn't take crap from anyone, and I think it hurt him in becoming the WWF world heavyweight champion.

For our match in L.A., the arena was packed with mostly Hispanic fans. I didn't know it at the time, but the company was going to have Paul beat me so that he would become champion. After he gave me a pile-driver, the Hispanic fans started throwing things in the ring. Paul was being pelted by oranges, cans, bottles, you name it. At first he just egged them on, but then he realized that things were truly bordering on pandemonium. In fact, a fan even got in the ring and jumped on Paul's back. He had to flee the ring because there was almost a full-fledged riot.

A few days later during a match in Erie, Pennsylvania, Paul locked me in a move that popped the cartilage in my knee. It was very painful and I couldn't walk or put pressure on my knee. André the Giant had to help me back to my hotel room that night. The following day I hobbled to the airport to catch a flight to the next town. I spoke to Roddy Piper, one of the most intelligent guys in the business, on the flight. He gave me some great advice, telling me to ask Vince to parlay the injury into an angle.

When I saw Vince later that day, he was shocked to see me on crutches. I asked him about doing an angle with Paul where he would injure my knee, leaving me shelved for a few months while allowing him to become the new champion. After having surgery and rehabbing my knee, I would return to against Paul to win my title back. Vince liked the idea so we ran with it. However, the program wasn't with Paul, it was with Valentine.

I nursed my knee back to where I thought I was in good enough shape to defend the title against Valentine at a TV taping in Toronto. I had my knee taped before my match and it felt great, but it was still a little tender. Greg was an excellent wrestler and experienced pro who got me in the ring and went to work on my knee right away. I fought as best as I could and was able to connect with a good flying forearm. I should have been able to pin Greg, but his manager, Captain Lou Albano, interfered. Greg got the upper hand again and illegally pinned me using the ropes. My knee was in so much pain at that point that it was

Greg Valentine and I battled frequently early in my career. He was on the losing end of this exchange. That's Jimmy Hart in the background.

throbbing. I knew I had been robbed of my title, but at that point I wanted to get out of the ring and find a doctor, quick.

As I was exiting the ring, Greg blindsided me once again, dragged me back onto the mat, and put his figure-four leg lock on me. Captain Lou kept the referee occupied and Greg used the top rope of the ring to pull himself up and apply extra pressure. I heard a really loud pop in my knee that I'm sure was audible to the fans at ringside. I knew I was in trouble. I had to be carried out on a stretcher, and all of a sudden my Intercontinental Title was the last of my worries. My future was in doubt.

Three days later I had knee surgery. Luckily, in surgery they found no significant ligament damage. My injury kept me out of action for just a couple of weeks. Still, I had to go through some very rigorous rehabilitation on my tendon. As an athlete my entire life, I managed the pain and did additional rehab at my home gym.

6

RECLAIMING MY BELT

FEUDING WITH THE HAMMER

With WrestleMania II right around the corner, the company pitted Greg Valentine and me in a rematch. I had been chasing Greg for over a year, trying to regain my belt, and the fans loved watching us go at each other. We gave our fans a great show every time, beating each other black and blue. After Greg had torn up my knee in '85, we began a long feud that lasted for over a year. During that time, we wrestled in all kinds of matches: lumberjack matches, taped-fist matches, hour-draw matches, no-time-limit matches, no-disqualification matches, and even one anything-goes steel-cage match in Baltimore.

The cage match was typical of our battles. We beat on

each other for 15 or 20 minutes. He ran my head into the steel cage and my forehead started bleeding. Before it was all over, though, he was bleeding worse than I was. His old scars caused him to bleed more, and it was easier to see the blood on him because of his blond hair. I didn't have many scars, so I didn't open up easily. That was fine with me: I didn't want any scars on my head. To make sure I avoided any unnecessary cuts, when the bookers asked me to blade, I did a very poor job at it. Eventually, they quit asking me to do it. If you look at my head today, there is only one scar. And that scar didn't come from a blade. In a match against Brutus "The Barber" Beefcake at the OMNI in Atlanta, he slammed my head into the side of the ring apron. The stiff blow busted me wide open, which resulted in 14 stitches.

I beat Greg in that steel-cage match to regain the Intercontinental Title. When I went back into the ring to accept the belt. Greg took it from the referee and smashed the belt into the cage, busting it into pieces. I was awarded the busted-up belt while on my knees, and I lifted it over my head in victory. The fans were cheering me on and it was a great feeling.

NEARLY BLIND LUCK

After I regained the title, I remained at my peak for a couple years. I had finally been established as a top wrestler and received world recognition as well as respect from many of my fellow wrestlers. I defended the Intercontinental Title against anybody and everybody, taking my lumps in the process.

One night at Madison Square Garden in a match against Paul Orndorff, I took a nasty spill. As I ran toward him and to try to land a flying forearm, he ducked at the last second. As he dropped down, he grabbed the top rope so I had nothing to grab onto as I went by. I flew over the top rope and out of the ring. I was able to turn in the air and land on the concrete floor on my back. My sweat caused me to slide and probably kept me from a real serious injury. Everyone watching thought I had killed myself, but I was relatively okay after a few days, lucky that I hadn't suffered a serious injury.

I will never forget my 1987 main-event match against Roddy Piper in Buffalo, New York, in front of a packed crowd. During our match, Piper accidentally stuck his finger in my eye. Although wrestlers compete against each other, we rarely try to harm each other. There are some exceptions, but in this case, Piper felt bad for his mistake. When I told him I couldn't see, he got worried. He kept apologizing and didn't touch me again until I regained my sight about three minutes later. During that time, he left me alone in the corner of the ring and kept the referee occupied. After the match, Piper was still apologizing. Luckily, I didn't suffer any long-term effects from the poke.

HAWAII OR BUST

Around this time, Vince asked me to cover a match in Hawaii for the Junkyard Dog. I had just worked for almost

30 days in a row without seeing my family, and I finally had two days off. My first day home, Vince Jr. called me and said, "Tito, you won a trip to Hawaii!" I told Vince I couldn't go because we were going to close on our first house. Vince said, "No problem."

After my two short days off, I called to get my bookings. Lo and behold, I had been demoted. Vince had pushed me down from the "A" team to the "C" team. Although I didn't do anything wrong, he punished me for the Junkyard Dog's unreliability. Aloha!

LIGHTS OUT FOR THE CHAMP

I won back the Intercontinental title in Baltimore and then lost it again in Boston eight months later to a newcomer by the name of Randy "Macho Man" Savage. Without a doubt, that 1986 match against Savage was a tough one. A capacity crowd at the old Boston Garden screamed like mad throughout the entire 20-minute match, which left both of us drenched in sweat. Miss Elizabeth, Randy's manager, was ringside for the match. She was a very beautiful woman who was adored by the fans. Randy used to mistreat her, and the fans hated Randy for that.

Toward the end of our match, Miss Elizabeth gave Randy a small piece of iron that resembled a dumbbell and fit perfectly over his fist. He hid it from both the referee and me, and as I was lifting him into the ring, he punched me in the forehead. It was lights out for me. The match was over and I lost the title.

At least this moment in the ring with the Macho Man wasn't embarrasing.

BARE BOTTOM

When I wrestled Randy Savage again to try to regain my belt, I did a move on him called a "Sunset Flip." As I bounced back off the ropes, he was bent over, facing me, in an effort to flip me into the air. But I jumped over him and grabbed his waist with my hands taking him down into a pin position. I didn't pin him, and later in the match he got back at me with that same move. As he flipped over me, he grabbed my trunks, pulling them down so my rear end was totally exposed. To say the least, I was real embarrassed.

A RUDE AWAKENING

That same year, 1986, during a TV taping in Nashville, I had a match against "Ravishing" Rick Rude that ended up almost as embarrassing as my Sunset Flip contest against Savage. Rick Rude's gimmick was his supposed sex appeal; his manager would invite women into the ring, and Rick would plant a big kiss on each. The kiss was his finishing move, which he called the "Rude Awakening."

After our Nashville match, which Rick won, he was getting ready to do his Rude Awakening on a beautiful female fan. This is when I decided I could do it just as well, if not better. I had left the ring, heading for the dressing room, when I suddenly turned and ran back into the ring. I knocked Rick out of the ring, and took the girl into my arms. I leaned her back as I held her and we kissed. It was supposed to be a slight bend, but I leaned too far forward. As I kissed her, we just kept going down, all the way to the mat. I ended up lying on top of her, which was embarrassing because I'd screwed up the move. But it turned out okay as the fans loved it. I had hoped that something more would come of it, but no such luck.

WRESTLEMANIA III

WrestleMania III took place in March 1987 at Detroit's Silver Dome in front of almost 100,000 people. It was an event loaded with great wrestling talent and plenty of celebrities, including rock star Alice Cooper, comedian Bob Uecker, and movie star Mary Hart. It was great wrestling

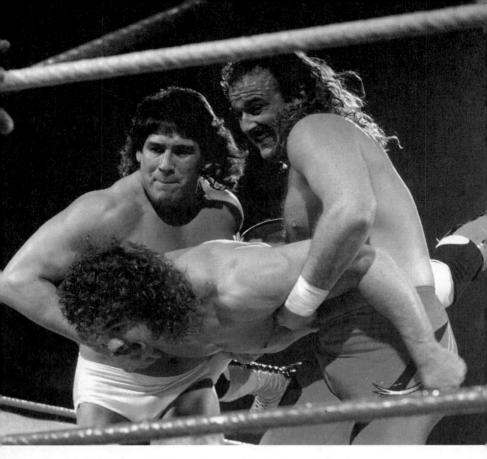

With a little help from Jake Roberts, I escort Rick Rude out of the ring.

event to be a part of, but I was very unhappy with my position. I ended up being part of a six-man, tag-team match. I tagged with the British Bulldogs against the Hart Foundation and Danny Davis.

Davis was initially just a very good referee with the company. Then Vince created an angle for Danny to become controversial referee, which I thought was a genius move. I never expected the fans to buy into the character, but Danny did such an outstanding job that they did. He essentially befriended the heels, helping them win matches.

That spearheaded his move from a referee to a wrestler.

The Bulldogs and I lost our nine-minute match after the Harts' manager, Jimmy Hart, hit Davey Boy on the head with his megaphone. Later in the show, I attacked and soon thereafter ripped the clothes off Butch Reed's manager, Slick.

This set up a shorter program between Butch and me. Since Ricky Steamboat was now the Intercontinental champion, Vince put Butch and me together to determine if eventually one of us would work our way up into contention for the belt. Butch and I had some very good matches over a two-month period. But our program was simply mid-card matches that didn't amount to too much for either of us.

HULK VS. ANDRÉ

The match that everyone came to see at WrestleMania III was the epic battle between champion Hulk Hogan, and challenger André the Giant. Although Hulk beat André, neither my fellow wrestlers nor I had any advance knowledge on the outcome of the match. Like the fans, we were in the dark, and excited to watch the match from backstage.

There seemed to be some jealousy and static between Hulk and André, which led to my belief that Hulk and André would never agree to put on such a stellar match. The friction existed because André had been *the man* for years, and a lot of the boys didn't think that André would accommodate Hulk and officially pass him the torch on national television. Although André and I were good friends, he never told me anything about the match, and I had enough respect for him to not pry. Despite the build-up for the biggest match in the history of the company, both wrestlers protected the match and kept their mouths shut.

I recall a host of guys—Brutus Beefcake, Jimmy Hart, Randy Savage, Ricky Steamboat, Bobby Heenan, myself, and others—glued to the TV monitor to catch the action. I personally didn't think André would sell a lot for Hulk, but boy was I totally wrong. He worked his tail off in the match. The climactic moment arrived when Hulk body-slammed the 500-pound André—the first time André had ever been slammed. There wasn't a single person in the locker room who trusted their eyes after watching that miraculous move. In the first place, André had a lot of physical problems; his ability to position himself in a manner to allow Hulk to lift him is a true testament to André's drive and ability. Nobody was going to do anything to André unless he wanted it done. Equally amazing is the fact that Hulk was physically able to body slam André. All of us watching let out a collective, "Wow!" It was a good slam, and I think Hulk hurt his back in the process.

When the match was over, all the boys congratulated both wrestlers on a job well done. Hulk hugged and thanked André for passing the torch. Their match went far beyond anybody's expectations and set a new standard for the league. The immense effort netted both men a whopping million dollars each! More importantly for the business, André helped get over Hulk Hogan. And with Hulk at the helm, he took professional wrestling to another level.

MEETING MIL

I first met Mexican wrestling legend Mil Máscaras while working for Paul Boesch, the promoter of the Houston territory, in my early years in the business. As the young guy, it was my responsibility to drive Máscaras from venue to venue. I idolized Mil, so it was an honor to chauffeur him around. I was like a kid in a candy store. Mil was known as the "man of a thousand masks" because he always wore a mask in the ring. He was one of the first Mexican wrestlers to make it big outside of his home country, and he was also one of the original high flyers.

One night after a show, we stopped at a local convenience store to get a six pack of beer. As we were driving out of town, Mil took off his mask. I had never seen his face and was totally shocked. He never took off his mask in the ring, or in the locker room. In fact, he often wore two masks, one over the other.

He was actually a good-looking man, which surprised me, because wrestlers who wore masks were usually unattractive. I wondered why he covered his face, but I never asked him. At the time, I didn't see myself as worthy enough to ask such a personal question of a superstar.

Over a decade later in 1987, Paul sold his promotion to Vince, which allowed Mil and I to team up in a great match against the Demolition tag team. We won the match, and it was truly an honor to be in the same ring with the wrestling legend.

RACISM IN THE RING

I first met Jesse "The Body" Ventura while wrestling in the AWA. We enjoyed many great matches wrestling each other. In particular, I recall a steel-cage match between Bruno Sammartino and me against Ventura and Adrian Adonis. We won the match, but Jesse was so popular at that time that the loss had little impact on him. He was a master in getting the most from the crowd with the least amount of work. He was a true credit to the business.

After his career ended due to injury, Jesse became a commentator for the WWF. On several occassions, he referred to me as "Chico" or a "taco vendor." It's easy for me to understand why such comments were viewed as discriminatory, but let me be clear in saying that Jesse is not a racist person. He never said those things to be malicious toward me. He was simply acting in a way that would help me get over with the fans. And he did a great job at it.

On the other hand, I did feel a lot of sincere prejudice and racism from guys like Ole Anderson and Dick Murdoch. In fact, Dick, who wrestled in the south during the 1980s using the persona "Captain Redneck," even showed me his KKK membership card. Their actions and words to me and about me were very insensitive and hurtful.

SEEKING EQUITY

When several of my wrestling peers started receiving their merchandising checks, my eyes nearly popped out of their sockets: some guys were getting quarterly checks in the neighborhood of $90,000. Those were the wrestlers who the league had decided to market with wrestling dolls and the like. My doll didn't come out until the third quarter of the year, so I wasn't among those receiving the big pay out. When my doll was released, I was expecting to get a big check as well, but I only got a total of $18,000. I pinched my nose to Arnold Skaaland, who was cutting the check, to let him know I thought it stunk. He gave me a breakdown that differed from what I soon heard—that the decision had been made to cut back our share of the profits. That rumor turned out to be true. The last thing the WWF wanted was for its wrestlers to become too wealthy and grow independent. Then they wouldn't be able to control them. The days of big pay-offs were gone.

LOSING INTEREST IN THE BUSINESS

Toward the end of 1987, I began making plans to get out of wrestling. By that point, I knew I was not part of the WWF's long-term plan, and did not want to hang around to be misused and miscast. I was slowly being fazed out of the main events as the company turned to fresh faces and new talents. It seemed inevitable that I would soon be a curtain jerker. My career was going nowhere; Vince gave it to me, and he took it away just as quickly.

To try to find another niche for myself in the business, I started announcing the matches for the Spanish-speaking audience. It was a good experience for me, but my heart was in performing, not broadcasting. So my family and I explored some business options outside of wrestling.

7

STRIKING BACK

A NEW PARTNER

Just when I thought my wrestling career was over in the WWF, I was given another opportunity in late 1987 to be in the main events and earn big money. Once again, I got my break because another wrestler was not able to handle the grind of the WWF. Rick Martel lost his partner, Tom Zenk, and Vince decided to put me in Tom's spot. It was not quite the comeback I had hoped for—I preferred going it alone—but in the WWF, only one wrestler wrote his own ticket, Hulk Hogan. I needed the position and the money, so I accepted the invitation without any reservation. Shortly thereafter, Rick and I became the babyface tag-team known simply as "Strike Force."

When I was first told about the tag-team, Vince suggested the name Border Patrol, which I didn't like. Earlier that year, several illegal immigrants crossing the border from Mexico had died in a boxcar along the Arizona border. It was all over the news. I told Vince, "If we use this name, we will immediately be a heel tag-team." Vince thought about it and agreed, and eventually we settled on Strike Force.

TAG-TEAM CHAMPIONS

I was determined to make our tag team successful. I knew Rick could carry his end, and I made sure that I carried my end. We enjoyed chemistry together and were very good in the ring, so the fans backed us from the start. We rode that momentum to the world tag-team championship belt, which we earned by defeating the Hart Foundation.

Being back in the spotlight reenergized my passion for wrestling. Our tag-team success led to Vince booking us at WrestleMania IV in Atlantic City. We were the second to last match of the evening, and Rick and I were paired in a title match against Demolition, which at that time consisted of Ax and Smash, both of whom were managed by Mr. Fuji. In wrestling, it makes more sense—and builds more excitement amongst fans—for the good guys to be in pursuit of a belt held by the bad guys, rather than the other way around. Thus, Rick and I lost our belts at WrestleMania IV. Ax used Mr. Fuji's cane to pop Rick on the back, then

Rick Martel and I enjoyed our time as tag-team champs.

roll him up for the victory.

The fans figured we were robbed from our belts, and they wanted us to win them back. That sense of moral justice rallied our fan base. Vince knew exactly what he was doing. He made his best money when good and evil feuded, and the fans sided with good. So, for the next few months we battled Demolition.

As a tag team, things went well for Strike Force for about two more years. We had feuds against the Hart Foundation and Demolition, as well as the Bolsheviks and the Islanders. Once again, due to an unfortunate situation, this run came to an end. An illness in Rick's family took him away from wrestling for nearly a year. I tried to talk him into working it out, but he decided it was more important for him to stay at home and tend to the sensitive situation. So, when Rick left, Strike Force was no more.

SURVIVING IN 1988

On Thanksgiving night in 1988, André the Giant, Rick Rude, Curt "Mr. Perfect" Hennig, Dino Bravo, and Harley Race defeated Ken Patera, Jake "The Snake" Roberts, "Hacksaw" Jim Duggan, Scott Casey, and me. I was eliminated by André after he sat—yes, sat—all 500 pounds of his body on my chest. I thought I was going to be crushed to death.

Almost 20 years later, four of the five wrestlers in that match who I fought against are dead. André was the only one who died of natural causes. Dino was murdered, and both Rick and Curt died from substance abuse. Something needs to be done to clean up the substance and drug abuse problems in wrestling. The abuse of steroids, pain killers, alcohol, and other drugs is damaging wrestlers and ending careers; sometimes lives.

QUITE THE REUNION

When Rick returned to the WWF, we reformed Strike Force, and the wrestling world was our oyster. We quickly regained momentum and earned a tag-team title shot against the Brain Busters at WrestleMania V in 1989. Tully Blanchard and Arn Anderson, collectively known as the Brain Busters, were a talented duo who were managed by the legendary Bobby "The Brain" Heenan. We had a great match full of fast-paced action and teamwork from both sides.

Around 15 minutes into the match, I accidentally bumped into Rick, which seemed to upset him, so I immediately apologized. To both me and the fans, Rick's reaction was very condescending. He thought I had hit him on purpose. I tried to explain myself, but before I knew it, Rick had left the ring and was headed back to the dressing room. That left me by myself to compete against both Tully and Arn. Even though I tried, I was no match for the both of them. I took a pretty good beating before they finally decided they had had enough fun with me. I was pinned after the Brain Busters delivered a spike piledriver.

Although I felt we had so much left to offer as a tag team, Vince turned Rick against me, thus ending Strike Force once and for all. Out of all this, I was the sacrificial lamb. I was used to turn Rick into an instant villain. He got a new gimmick and a fresh start as a solo wrestler called "The Model." That set me up for my revenge. We would feud for a while, and I made some good money during the process.

KING OF THE RING

In October 1989, I became the "King of the Ring" at the Providence Civic Center in Rhode Island. In the fifth

annual tournament, I defeated—in order—Bad News Brown, the Warlord, Akeem, and finally Rick Martel. In my third King of the Ring appearance, I joined the ranks of other wrestling legends who had won the event, including Ted DiBiase, The Macho Man, and Harley Race. At that time, however, the event wasn't of much significance. It wasn't a big-time pay-per-view event and there was no ceremony for the winner. It was just another in a long line of shows.

LEFT OUT AGAIN

By 1989, Vince's desires for the WWF continued to evolve. He wanted all of his wrestlers to have a more muscular look, and he felt that my look was no longer sufficient. He began to move me to the sideline. That rejection hurt me, but forced me to finally accept the fact that in the wrestling business there was no such thing as loyalty. I worked out hard and lifted weights, stayed away from drugs, and didn't get into any trouble. I did what the company told me and never disrespected my profession. Yet all of this meant little. In the end, Vince was all about making money and looking to the future, not the past. He had a vision for the WWF, and that vision did not include me.

Once Strike Force was disolved, Rick and I went back to being enemies in the ring.

By early 1990, I was so unhappy—my pay cut in half—that I was again ready to give it all up. At a TV taping in Toledo, Ohio, I told Vince that I was ready to finish up my career and leave the company. After exchanging pleasantries and thanking him for the good times, I let him know that I was simply unhappy. I told Vince that I had discussed everything with my wife, and that my mind was made up to leave the company and move on with my life.

Well, I guess the good Lord was in that room with me that day. After listening to my reasons, Vince unexpectedly told me that he was not finished with me yet. Using an imaginary sliding scale to explain my value to the WWF, he explained to me that my career had always found me in the top half of the scale. He had never brought me below the halfway mark. That was not his intention.

He continued by telling me of his new idea to create a fresh character for me—"The Matador." The character would continue to play up my ethnic roots and appeal to the Hispanic demographic, while giving me a chance to rise to stardom in a new role. The idea sounded like a good opportunity to me.

The Matador actually originated in the mind of Dick Ebersol, who used to produce the *Saturday Night Main Event* for us. Well before this meeting with Vince, Dick had told me that he had suggested the gimmick to Vince. If Vince had acted on Dick's suggestion at that time, it wouldn't have been Vince's great idea, but Dick's. By the time Vince suggested the idea to me, Dick was gone, making the idea all his.

Vince told me to learn as much as I could about real-life matadors, but to keep the idea between the both of us for the time being. I did as I was told, going to the public library in my free time to research matadors and prepare for my rebirth in the WWF.

STILL TITO, FOR NOW

While I was studying to become El Matador, I continued to wrestle as Tito Santana. Every three weeks, at the TV tapings, I would ask Vince whether the time was right to launch the character. Vince always had a good excuse to put me off. Clearly, The Matador was not his top priority.

I kept wrestling, but was demoted to the very bottom of the pecking order. Vince made it clear that when I came in as El Matador, I would be a brand new character that he could build into a superstar. But after six months had passed, I was still wrestling solely as Tito, and I had my doubts.

Finally, I was informed in October 1990 that the upcoming Survivor Series would be my last match as Tito Santana. I went out with a bang, winning the opening-round match by eliminating Boris Zhukov and Tanaka (one half of The Orient Express tag team) following flying forearms. I moved on to the Grand Finale after Sgt. Slaughter was disqualified. In the final match, I eliminated The Warlord before being eliminated myself by my old buddy, Ted DiBiase.

On the night of the taping, I also found out from the

office that my final phase of training for the matador gimmick would be held in Spain. The WWF was sending me to an actual school for matadors, which meant I would end up in a real bullfight. Unfortunately, things didn't work out for my trip to Spain, so instead I was sent to a training organization in Mexico City.

8

EL MATADOR

TRAVELING THE WORLD

By 1991, the WWF had begun to branch out into Europe, organizing tours there a couple times a year. It was a brand new market for us, one that made lots of money for Vince. The huge European arenas would sell out in a matter of hours.

My matador training in Mexico was postponed, so I was sent to Europe for seven days in April 1991. I performed as Tito Santana, wrestling in London, Manchester, Berlin, Brussels, and Barcelona. It was a nice trip, but very unfulfilling for me as I was wrestling in preliminary matches of little consequence. I didn't get a chance to do any sight seeing, either. The younger guys went barhopping every night, but I just couldn't keep up. Rest was more important to me. It was just too hard for me to have fun and relax when my future was so uncertain.

In early May, I went to Japan for another week of wrestling. J.J. Dillon, an ex-wrestler who had retired from the ring, was a sort of acting foreign ambassador for the WWF. He'd been around about 20 years and had also managed other wrestlers, most notably the Four Horsemen faction. Despite his experience, Dillon had the worst personality. To be blunt, it was tough for him to be nice to anyone, which made him a puzzling choice to represent the league.

Dillon informed me after the tour of Japan that I would next travel to Tijuana, Mexico, in less that two weeks to start my matador schooling. It was a huge relief to know that I would finally be able to complete my transformation to El Matador and begin to work the gimmick.

MATADOR IN TRAINING

Deep down, I wasn't very comfortable with becoming a gimmick wrestler, since I had spent so much of my career wrestling as a normal guy. But if that's what the boss wanted, I would go along with it. In Mexico, I learned as much as I could about the matador from a man named Maestro Jesus. He was a very small man, but had been a matador nearly all of his adult life. He was a very patient instructor, which I appreciated.

I practiced all the techniques of a matador, using man-

I took my matador training seriously, but I wasn't about to train with a live bull.
Photo courtesy of Tito Santana

made bulls as my opponents. I studied maneuvers with the cape and banderoles, which are the two lances a matador sticks into the bull's neck before finally using a sword to kill the animal. By my third day there, an actual bullfight was put on with a crowd and an amateur matador as my stunt double. The vignettes were pieced together for TV in a way that made it appear as if I were the one fighting the bull. The event drew a good crowd, and afterward I went through a procession with other matadors in which we were introduced to the fans. Of course, I wanted to take a few passes at the bulls, but Vince McMahon made it clear that he did not want me to take a chance. So I did not get too close to the bulls. From what I saw, they were a scary sight.

I have always admired matadors, who are greatly skilled and fearless men. My dad took the family to two bullfights when I was young. I remember being in awe of the matadors, who are considered heroes in Mexico and Spain. But now that I'm older, I just don't see the sport in killing a tired bull. It's simply inhumane.

With my training complete, it was time to see if wrestling fans, many of whom had appreciated me as Tito Santana, would take to El Matador in the same way.

MY DEBUT BECAME SID'S DEBUT

El Matador was supposed to be introduced at the 1991 SummerSlam, but that didn't happen. Shortly before the event, I was told that another superstar in the making by the name of Sid Justice was also making his debut. It wouldn't be fair for either one of us, the WWF told me, if we were both making our debut on the same night. So I had to wait while Sid, a huge wrestler at about 6-foot-10 and 340 pounds, made his debut.

Sid had a reputation for a bad temper that preceded him, hence his nickname Sycho Sid. Vince had been warned about Sid's hostile behavior by Hulk and a few others, but Vince thought he could tame him. So he gave Sid the royal treatment at SummerSlam. Sid could have been the one to replace Hulk Hogan—the two fought each other in WrestleMania VIII—but he stuck around for less than a year before getting fed up and quitting for reasons unclear. The WWF had everyone thinking that he had just walked out. Then we found out through the grapevine he had been suspended for testing positive for steroids. Sid's manager, Harvey Wippleman, confided in me that it was indeed a positive steroids test that had caused his departure.

Sid went back to the WCW, where he had come from prior to joining the WWF; but he didn't last long there, either. He was fired after getting into a seriously bloody fight in a hotel room with Arn Anderson. Sid had just gotten a big contract, and after a few beers he began bragging about his money. Arn, who was more experienced than Sid but had never made that kind of money, took it hard. One of them hit the other with a chair across the head, and somehow that led to a stabbing involving a pair of scissors.

Sid later returned to the WWF, but he never became a star like Hogan.

EL MATADOR VIGNETTES

About three weeks after SummerSlam '91, Dillon told me my time had come. I was ecstatic that I would finally have the chance to introduce the matador gimmick to wrestling fans. I filmed two 30-second vignettes, both directed by Vince. In the first, I talked about the origins of El Matador. My second vignette showed me entering the arena, while reflecting upon my fans, the bulls I had challenged, and my future. My transition to El Matador was an easy transition for fans to accept for one primary reason: I remained Tito Santana. I didn't transform into a foreign character; instead, I just added the "El Matador" tag to my name—Tito Santana, El Matador.

In the third vignette, we brought a bull into the arena. My trainer explained the dangers of the horns and the bull's ability to inflict severe harm. He explained to me that the more danger that was involved, the more bullfighting fans appreciated the matador. The following week we released another vignette that focused on the advanced training that I had gone through to become a matador. Wrestling fans witnessed my mounting confidence as I practiced on a mechanical bull that charged me. As I eluded the bull, I stuck him with a pair of banderoles on the back of the neck. My trainer drove home the point that one simple mistake could be my last. He also praised my agility, noting that most matadors were small men; that I was so talented at my size was an accomplishment.

We put a lot of time and effort in the fifth vignette. In this particular one, I was shown completing my training and returning to my fictional hometown in Tijuana, Mexico, where I would perform in front of my own people. A fiesta was held to celebrate the event. In the sixth and final vignette, I was shown fighting an actual bull. Of course, the piece was edited to make it appear as if I were battling the beast, but I was not. The vignettes worked out better than I had ever expected. The fans, after following my extensive training, were ready to get behind me.

MY "HOMETOWN"

When I wrestled as Tito Santana, ring announcer Howard Finkel always announced to the fans that I was from "Tocula" Mexico. There is no such town by this name in Mexico. He was supposed to say "Toluca," but for some reason Howard couldn't pronounce it correctly. After several attempts to correct him, I finally gave up. He did, however, later get Tijuana right.

WILL EL MATADOR SURVIVE?

November 1, 1991 was established as the new debut date for El Matador. For my first match, I wrestled the late Hercules Hernandez. We were pitted against each other several times during my initial tour. Hercules was an old veteran and people liked him, so it was tough for him to play the role of a heel. The fans also wondered if I was going to remain a babyface or turn heel. I remained a good guy, a trait that I maintained through my entire career—a rarity for a wrestler.

My first few matches in Pittsburgh, Milwaukee, and Moline, Illinois, were tough. Not until my fourth night in Denver did I get a good response from the crowd. I had been putting a lot of effort into the character but had yet to receive the big push that Vince had promised me. There was no way El Matador was going anywhere with that push.

The positive reception from fans continued while touring in California. The reaction from the predominately Hispanic crowd in both Oakland and San Diego reassured me that I was on track for success. But I was still not getting much play on TV, and there was little in the way of merchandise. That let me know where I stood with Vince.

I was upset. I thought about pushing the issue with Vince, but I was tired of fighting him and simply just let it go. Besides, I knew that fighting him further on the issue of merchandise wasn't going to do me any good. Around this time, I was summoned for a deposition by Bill Eadie, who was suing Vince. Bill had been part of a successful tag team called Demolition, in which he wrestled as Ax and partnered with Smash. Demolition split up around 1990, and Bill became just one of many wrestlers who had been more or less forced to quit the WWF. He moved on to the independent circuit, but he soon found a reason to bring the fight back to the WWF. Promises had been made to Bill that weren't kept, and he wanted some justice. The WWF had stopped paying him residuals from the merchandising of his dolls, games, and tapes. From my recollection, I don't think Bill recovered anything from Vince.

I didn't figure I'd have any more luck.

I waited a long time for my debut as El Matador.

9

THE WILD WWF

SCANDALOUS

The WWF overcame some unreal obstacles during my stint with the league. Lawyers must have made a fortune off the league in order to keep a lot of potential scandals from erupting. It seemed to me like every month brought with it a new scandal. If you stop to think about it, that is really not surprising. There were at least 60 wrestlers on the road at any given time. Many of those wrestlers were on a big-time ego trip and hopped up on drugs, booze, or steroids. One can imagine the sort of havoc we could wreak. As hard as we were working in the ring, our vices were often working double-time outside the ring in an effort to keep our robotic professional lives from wearing us down.

The range of scandals the league faced was staggering, from allegations of homosexual activities to office personnel accused of transporting minors across state lines. Vince was linked in a sex scandal with a female referee. A group of wrestlers appeared on TV shows with Geraldo Rivera and Phil Donahue stating that certain higher ups at the WWF demanded sexual favors for career advancement. Worst of all, Vince had been accused of distributing steroids to his wrestlers. There was enough going on to fill up the tabloids twice over.

Early in 1992, on my way to California for an 11-day tour, I learned that Hulk Hogan was under fire from the national media. The topic: steroids. Two other wrestlers—Superstar Billy Graham and "Dr. D," David Schultz—were guests on a TV talk show. Speaking about steroids and its use in professional wrestling, Graham and Schultz threw the Hulkster under the bus, pinning all the blame on him.

As a fellow wrestler, it was amusing to watch it all unfold. But I had to feel sorry for Hulk. As successful as he had become, the man had a good heart and he cared for other people. He had done a lot to help Graham and Schultz earn a living in wrestling by carrying the league, and so many of its wrestlers, on his shoulders for so long. He is the only WWF wrestler who was worth every cent he received. But as the WWF's leading man, he also was the obvious choice for the national media to pick on.

CALLED TO TESTIFY

On February 15, 1994, I received a call from Vince's secretary asking me to contact Vince's lawyers. The FBI had been investigating Vince for about two years in relation to steroids in the WWF, and his role in the matter. He was scheduled to go to trial in May. I had heard lots of rumors, including that Hulk was supposed to be the FBI's main witness in its case against Vince.

In deposition I was asked, "Has Vince ever asked you, or anyone else, to take any steroids?" My answer was "No." I told the lawyers that when I was part of "Strike Force," I went up to Vince myself and asked if I should be doing anything else to improve my body. His answer was "No, you look fine." I also told the lawyers that Vince had brought up steroids in one of our general meetings, telling all of us that we didn't need to use steroids, that our positions within the WWF weren't determined by appearances.

The lawyers were after the truth, period. They pressed me about steroids, and I told them over and over, "No, I never took them—and Vince never asked me to use them." In the end, I never testified in court, and Vince was rightfully acquitted of all charges.

DRUG TESTING

Vince did get tougher in dealing with steroid and drug use in the early to mid-1990s. He created an in-house company that started randomly testing us for illegal drugs, excluding steroids. He sent a few guys to rehab, but for some, no amount of intervention helped. I sincerely believe that this testing alone, if enforced sooner, could have helped save some guys' lives and marriages. Certain wrestlers will never admit it, but I do believe that some owe Vince a thank you for taking extra measures to try to get the WWF's drug problems under control.

Later on, Vince instituted testing for steroid use. Big bodies were in, so guys were doing whatever they had to do to build up their appearances. At first, steroids were not illegal. But even after they became illegal, some wrestlers felt obligated to use them. Even though Vince was sold on big bodies, I never heard him tell a wrestler to take steroids, as some have claimed.

Despite the WWF's efforts—the league even hired the number-one doctor in the drug-testing business—the drug problem didn't go away. Initially, the tests were easy to beat. If a guy was concerned about failing his test, he would get a clean friend to pee in a bottle for him. When it came time to take a urine sample, the wrestler would use his friend's sample instead of his own. As time went on, the league got wise to such tricks. Eventually, they made us drop our pants and someone would watch us from beginning to end. In addition, the league began randomly testing, sometimes as often as two or three times a week.

Vince took this matter seriously, as he was on a crusade to repair the league's public image. He did not want another scandal to ruin his big business. Steroid and cocaine use would get a wrestler a six-week suspension. A second failed test meant a rehab program, and a third failed test meant the end of the line. For marijuana, the first offense was a $1,000 fine, followed by fines of $3,500 and $5,000.

I kept myself clean because I didn't want to embarrass my family. I couldn't see blowing money on drugs. Some guys spent up to $1,000 or more per week on enhancement drugs. I worked too hard for my money, and my family meant too much to me to blow my career just to try and get a perceived edge. I also felt good about being a positive role model.

Despite Vince's best efforts—for a while he seemed to have matters under control—there is still today a publicized drug problem in professional wrestling. Vince is right when he says he isn't responsible for what someone does when they leave the ring. How can anyone hold a promoter responsible for what a wrestler does in the privacy of his or her own home? That said, it seems as if in today's WWF only the muscle-heads are getting the big push. The wrestling fan now expects to see an overly muscular wrestler. It's a shame what the business has come to. Back in my day, it didn't take a brain surgeon to figure out that the guys with the better bodies were usually more aggressively promoted. But the WWF also had its share of guys who had a different look, whether they be fat, skinny, balding, hairy, you name it. That diversity was a reflection of society, and the fans bought into the reality of the characters.

As the league currently stands today, I would not advise my worst enemy to become a professional wrestler, let alone my own children or the children that I teach.

RUMORS

By the early 1990s, rumors of homosexuality were running rampant in the company. I heard rumors that there were several homosexuals and bisexuals within the office, but I don't know how much truth there was to any of them. The *New York Post* printed an article that stated that some of the WWF's front-office personnel had been transporting minors across state lines who were hired for sexual favors. Also, there were accusations of young wrestlers being asked to participate in homosexual activities in order to advance their careers. There was even a lady referee who accused Vince of making inappropriate advances.

Allegations were also leveled on Vince from his former limousine driver, James Stewart, who had been fired several months earlier. Stewart claimed that Vince himself went out looking for boys. None of these rumors ever proved to be true. Plenty of people have tried to catch Vince breaking the law, but no one has succeeded. Still, all the bad publicity hurt the business a lot in my eyes.

CAN YOU HEAR ME NOW?

Two friends of mine, Paul Orndorff and Tony Atlas, had a disagreement outside the ring and got into a fight. Paul took a bite out of Tony's ear and bit it right off! The argument stopped there. Paul took Tony to the hospital so Tony's ear could be stitched back on.

If I had to do it all over again, maybe I'd been a little "tougher" outside the ring . . . but not that tough.

KING TONGA VS. THE POLICE

Not all wrestlers get their injuries inside the ring. One night in St. Louis, I saw King Tonga (Haku) try to break up a bar fight. Breaking up other peoples' fights was often how King Tonga ended up in fights himself. On this particular night, a bouncer hit King Tonga in the back of the head with a chair. For someone like King Tonga, who weighed over 300 pounds and had studied to become a sumo wrestler, this hardly fazed him. All it did was make him mad. He ended up hurting a few guys that night. He was squirted with mace by a policeman, which made him even madder. He took it out on a couple cops before finally deciding to give up.

The police handcuffed him and delivered a few blows with their nightsticks. In fact, this big cop smacked King Tonga across the head with his nightstick. King Tonga just shook his head and then stared just at the cop. He was taken in and locked up for a few hours.

I was sharing a room with King Tonga that night, and when he finally rolled in around 6:30 that morning, he looked awful. His face was burned and blistered from the mace, and his ankles, wrists, and shins were black and blue from the handcuffs. I cleaned his face with peroxide, punctured his blisters, cleaned them up, and covered his face with Neosporin. He applied ice to his body in several spots to ease the swelling. He was clearly hurting.

The worst part was that I had to wrestle him that night. I don't know how he survived.

LOOKING FOR A FIGHT

I almost got into a fight one day with Shawn Michaels. On a flight to Glasgow, Scotland, Shawn and I were both assigned to the same seat. I was there first and had gone to the lavatory. When I came back, Shawn was settling down in my seat. I politely asked him if he would mind moving so I could sit down, since I had already claimed the seat. He got up and moved, but then came back a few moments later wanting to start an argument. He snapped at the wrong guy, because I was not in the mood to take any crap that day. Shawn quieted down when I told him I would kick his butt, and after we landed we made up. So everything was cool.

We were like kids in a way, arguing and fighting with each other all the time. We usually laughed it off in the morning—but not always. At a 1988 event in Peoria, Illinois, Dan Spivey and Adrian Adonis really went at one another. Adonis had been ribbing Spivey for days and Spivey finally had enough. During their match, Spivey knocked Adonis out with a big right. To stop the match, he then gave the referee a shove, which disqualified him. Spivey walked back to the dressing room. After he recovered, Adonis went looking for Spivey. Adonis was in the wrong, but he didn't know when to stop. He started another fight with Spivey in the dressing room, and again Adonis was knocked down several times. With a cut over eye that was badly bleeding, Adonis was finally dragged out of the room.

"THE MONTREAL SCREWJOB"

On November 9, 1997, at the Survivor Series in Montreal, Shawn Michaels became the WWF Heavyweight champion for the third time—but not without controversy. Michaels defeated Bret Hart in what is today considered the most-talked-about, real-life double-cross in the history of the business. I was ringside in Montreal that night doing the color commentary for the WWF's Spanish announcing team. I think the entire incident should have never, ever occurred.

Vince saw a lot of potential in Shawn, and so he naturally wanted Shawn to be the titleholder. But Bret had a unique contract with certain stipulations written into it, namely that he had the creative control to say he could not lose a match in his home country of Canada. The two wrestlers had been feuding with each other for a while. Shawn wanted some finality to the bickering and constant struggle, so he went to Vince prior to the Montreal match and gave him an ultimatum: "Either Bret goes or I go."

I was just as shocked as everyone else when referee Earl Hebner called for the bell that ended the match after Shawn put Bret in Bret's own finisher, the Sharpshooter, even though Bret never submitted. I remember thinking that something was wrong, because the ending didn't make sense. I could even see the confusion in Bret's eyes. There was no way Bret would have tapped out that quickly.

The swerve was Vince's plan all along. He was ringside and ordered that the bell be rung. A pissed-off Bret spit in Vince's face at ringside, and then went crazy outside the ring, destroying TV monitors and other equipment. Triple

H and Jerry Brisco escorted Michaels back to the dressing room as the Canadian crowd roared in disapproval. I thought at the time that maybe this was all just part of an angle, because I would have never expected Bret to conduct himself in such a way if it wasn't planned.

After the match, tensions boiled over backstage. The British Bulldog told me that Vince followed Bret to the locker room and tried to cordially explain the situation. Bret wasn't in the mood to listen and told Vince that he was taking a shower, and if Vince knew what was good for him he better not hang around. For whatever reason, Vince stuck around and Bret clocked him. Vince never threw a punch. The rest is history.

For all these years, I never thought Shawn was in on the swerve. I couldn't believe it when he revealed in his autobiography that he (as well as Triple H and Brisco) was indeed in on the swerve. I couldn't believe it because at the time he acted and talked like he had no idea why Vince screwed Bret.

From what I understand, Bret *was* willing to lose his belt to Shawn, just not in his homeland of Canada. Nothing personal, but I think Bret was wrong and overreacted in an unprofessional manner. Vince giveth, and he taketh away. That's the nature of the business.

MARTY THE PRANKSTER

Marty Jannetty had a great personality and was a very likeable guy. But he did like to pull pranks. On one particular plane flight, a group of wrestlers, including me, were sitting near a loud-mouthed guy. This guy had clearly been drinking too much, and he began insulting all the wrestlers. Before we landed, he finally shut up when he fell asleep. That was a big mistake. When the poor guy woke up, he was greeted to a sickly smell. Marty had left the stranger a gift—Marty's lunch, digested—in his lap.

This stranger was irate, of course. He verbally threatened to shoot whichever wrestler had done him wrong. Security was alerted to the situation, and they detained the guy, who it turned out had just recently been released from a federal prison. When security searched his luggage, lo and behold they found a loaded gun!

On another plane flight, Marty sat next to three college kids who were bragging about how much they could party. Calling their bluff, Marty gave them all a drug called GHB, then a legal powder used by bodybuilders to burn body fat. Taking GHB on an empty stomach would knock a person right out, which is precisely what happened to these partiers. When they came to, their eyebrows had been shaved and half their head had received a bad hair cut, compliments of Marty.

KING POOP

In January 1993, the Royal Rumble was held at the Arco Arena in Sacramento, California. I was a participant in the event and was eliminated by the eventual winner, Yokozuna.

Jerry "The King" Lawler was also an entrant in the Rumble. He was despised at the time by a number of wrestlers, a fact that was made clear at the Rumble. Jerry couldn't wear his crown to the ring at the event, because someone had pooped in it. Several guys had a reason to do it, but no one took the credit. After the incident, we all received memos with our paychecks that fines would be enforced if we were caught in the prank. We still thought it was pretty funny.

WELCOME TO NYC

I will never forget the second time that Kerry Von Erich had ever been to New York. We had an evening bout scheduled at Madison Square Garden. While I got ready in the dressing room, Kerry walked in and told me about his afternoon. "Tito, you are never going to believe this," he said excitedly. "While I was taking in the sites around 42nd street, I heard a woman scream that someone had just stolen her purse. I turned around and I saw this guy running toward me with a gun in one hand and a purse in the other. When he got close enough to me, I gave him a clothesline and knocked him to the ground. Then I put my weight on him and waited for the police to arrive. They showed up within minutes and arrested him. The lady was ecstatic."

Kerry Von Erich didn't back down from anyone.

I just laughed and told Kerry, "Welcome to New York."

As he changed into his gear for the show, I noticed from the corner of my eye that he was grinning like a cheshire cat. He had no concerns about whether that guy could have shot him; he was just happy to be the hero. That was Kerry being Kerry. He was just such a nice guy and he genuinely cared for others.

SLEEPING AROUND

Max Moon had been around wrestling for years but never got the big break. We were good friends, until he crossed the line and began an affair with another wrestler's wife. I lost a lot of respect for him because of that. The funny thing is, the other wrestlers were more upset about the incident than the husband. A group of wrestlers made it rough for Max to stick around, constantly ribbing him. One time on a bus trip in Europe, The Nasty Boys started singing about how everyone's wives were safe back home in the States because Max Moon was on the bus with us. After the affair became public knowledge, Max's bookings decreased until he was left with no work.

NO-SHOWS

I wrestled with injuries, illnesses, personal problems, and the like for much of my career. But I've always given it 110 percent. In my career, I only missed two major appearances in 11 years. The first was to bring my wife home from the hospital after giving birth to our second son in 1984; the second happened a few months later when I was stranded at an airport due to a blizzard.

My peers in the WWF were not always so diligent about showing up to work. Toward the end of my career, the league suffered a rash of no-shows; some wrestlers simply weren't dependable. A good example is Shawn Michaels and his tag-team partner, Marty Jannetty. Marty and Shawn were making waves as "The Rockers" and had a great future ahead of them. Unfortunately, they were also young and wild. They were very talented as wrestlers, but they partied hard on many occasions and would miss their show the following day or night as a result.

SMUGGLING DRUGS

The Iron Sheik was a good man, but he had a serious drug problem. I know for a fact that a lot of promoters wouldn't deal with him because of his problem. Like anyone with a drug problem, the Sheik was bound to get into trouble. On a flight, I recall the Iron Sheik slipping some marijuana into another wrestler's carry-on bag. The other wrestler looked clean, so the Sheik figured that the wrestler would never be searched. The Sheik himself had a criminal record, having been busted for cocaine several years earlier. He had also failed a couple of the league's drug tests, and had been suspended and put into rehab. Luckily for both the Sheik and the other wrestler, no one got busted with the marijuana. But the Sheik's problems continued to follow up until he was eventually let go by the WWF.

HILLBILLY LIKES HIS RADAR

I almost ended up in jail because of Hillbilly Jim. Lanny Poffo and I were riding with Hillbilly to an event in Canada when he got pulled over for speeding. Hillbilly didn't hide the fact that he had a radar detector, and the cop confiscated the illegal detector. Hillbilly did not want to part with it, so he told the officer he would rather go to jail. As Lanny and I just sat there amazed, we listened to Hillbilly curse the police officer, who just happened to be a woman. Despite the insults and profanity, the officer refused to take us to jail. Lanny and I breathed a sigh of relief as the cop issued us a ticket, and more importantly, held on to the radar detector. The ticket cost us $60 each, but at least I didn't have to spend any time in the slammer.

HOCUS POCUS

On the flight back from a show, George "The Animal" Steele performed one of his notorious magic tricks on a beautiful flight attendant. She placed her open palm out,

I had to keep an eye on my luggage if I was sharing a flight with the Iron Sheik.

and George put a foam ball in her hand. He motioned for her to close it, which she did. He then tapped her hand, and she opened it to find two foam balls in her hand. The flight attendant was amazed. George again motioned for her to close her hand. She did as she was told, and he tapped her hand a second time. She opened her hand, but this time, she blushed with embarrassment. In her hand were not only two balls, but also a foam penis!

FAMILY AFFAIR

In late 1991, I teamed with Chavo Guerrero Sr. to battle Gino Hernandez and Tully Blanchard in an AWA match that happened to be in Houston. During the course of the match, I was thrown over the ropes and fell down hard on the concrete floor. Gino climbed out of the ring and began putting the boots to me. As I sold his kicks for the audience, I noticed that a lady was hitting Gino. I could't see her face, and I didn't think anything of it at the time. Shortly thereafter, the match ended in a disqualification for Gino and Tully, the heel team.

When I got back to the dressing room, Gino said to Tully, "I can't believe it! As I was putting the boots to Tito, this fat Mexican girl was slapping me in the back." He was livid as he showed me the marks on his back. I just thought it was another rowdy fan overexcited by the realistic picture that we were painting. After I cleaned up, I met my family at a local restaurant for dinner. My mom, brother, sister, aunt, and her family had all drove up that evening to watch me wrestle. As we were eating, my brother told me that my sister had hit Gino during my match. All of a sudden, I put two and two together. The big Mexican girl that Gino was talking about was my sister. I told my family how Gino was complaining about such a girl in the locker room. My sister said, "Yes, it was me. I was mad at him for kicking you." We all had a good laugh, but I continued to protect the business.

Another time, I wrestled AWA champion Nick Bockwinkel to a 60-minute draw. My 300-pound brother, who was in attendance to watch the show, ran into the ring when the referee raised my hand. Since my brother wasn't smart to the business, he thought I had won the belt and had become the new AWA champ. He picked me up and started hugging and squeezing me. I had just wrestled nonstop for 60 minutes and was completed exhausted. I had to scream at him to put me down and let go, because I could barely breathe.

Almost simultaneously security came into the ring to drag him away. I told security, "No, no. It's okay. He is my brother. He can stay." When the announcer told the crowd that a title doesn't change on a draw, and that Nick was still the champion, my brother was heartbroken and in tears. Once again, I said nothing and told my brother, "Don't worry. I'll get him next time."

10

CAST OF CHARACTERS

ONE WOMAN YOU DIDN'T WANT TO MESS WITH

Sensational Sherri was a very successful female wrestler and as tough as any man I have ever known. She was the only woman wrestler to work in all five of the major wrestling companies: WWF, NWA, AWA, WCW, and ECW. She held the WWF women's championship belt and was inducted in the WWF Hall of Fame in 2006.

At one point in her life, she was married to a Puerto Rican man who physically abused her. She told me she got fed up with him and beat him to a pulp with a frying pan and an iron. She left the guy on the floor of the house to die. Because of the experience with her ex-husband, Sherri didn't like too many Hispanics. But we respected each other and soon became friends. Whenever I saw her, I would tease her a lot and make light of her dislike for Hispanics. Sometimes I would jokingly ogle her and say, "Oh baby!" She would always respond with a smile, "Chico, never in a million years!"

Her troubles in life led her to drugs, and in 2007 she died of a drug overdose at the age of 49.

NAILZ

Nailz was an ex-con character created for the WWF by Vince. One day Nailz, whose real name was Kevin Wacholz, had a grueling argument with Vince that ended with Nailz taking Vince down and choking him. I happened to overhear the whole thing. The gist of it is Nails felt he was being underpaid, and I guess lacked the skills to verbally communicate his frustration to Vince. Although he was very inexperienced in the ring, Nailz had no problem acting the part of a ex-convict, because he actually was one.

I remember as the argument reached its peak, all of a sudden Nailz hollered, "He grabbed my balls!" The next thing I heard was Sergeant Slaughter and The Berzerker going in the room to break up the fight. Needless to say, that was the end of Nailz in the WWF. Wacholz filed a series

Although I got along with her well, Sensational Sherri was not someone you wanted as your enemy.

of lawsuits against Vince and the WWF, and testified against Vince in the steroids probe, too.

THE SNAKE

Jake "The Snake" Roberts was one of the greatest minds and performers in professional wrestling history. His gimmick, the huge python named Damien he carried into the ring with him in a canvas sack, was brilliant. Unfortunately, Jake left the WWF because of a misunderstanding with Vince. Jake wanted to spend less time on the road and more time at home with his family, which is simply not possible for a WWF wrestler. It's all or nothing, which is why a big percentage of wrestlers end up divorced.

BEFRIENDING THE
TEXAS TORNADO

When I started in professional wrestling, I knew very little about the major players in the profession. Simply put, I wasn't a fan. In early 1977, David Von Erich and I worked together in Joe Blanchard's territory. But it wasn't until I spent some years in the business that I realized how huge the Von Erich name was in wrestling. Later, when I worked in Atlanta, André the Giant, Kerry Von Erich, and I temporarily stayed with each other in an apartment. Kerry and I became good friends. Although he was only in the Atlanta territory for a few months, when Kerry left he told me that I was always welcome in his father's Dallas territory, World Class Championship Wrestling. I eventually got to know all the Von Erichs and found them all to be really nice guys. But Kerry was my favorite.

The story of Kerry's family is a sad one. It's hard to image, but Kerry lost four brothers: two by suicide, one by drugs, and a fourth by electrocution at a young age. As a parent, I can't imagine how Kerry's parents could have dealt with such losses. Kerry's life was never an easy one. He got involved in drugs at a young age, then was involved in a serious motorcycle accident that eventually required the amputation of his right foot. Thanks to an artificial foot, which he kept a secret for a while, he was able to continue wrestling.

When Kerry came to the WWF in 1990, we rekindled our friendship, often working out together. In early July 1992, Vince told me that I'd be in SummerSlam because Kerry, who was nicknamed "The Texas Tornado," had been fired. From what I remember of Kerry's time in the WWF, he was always under heavy medication. He told me of the constant pain he felt and the amount of morphine he needed to deal with it. His wife left him, which only escalated his emotional problems. He needed help, but no one stepped up to provide it. He was fired for too many no-shows and because he wouldn't—or couldn't—stop taking pain relievers. Drugs got the best of him. He ended his life by shooting himself at his dad's farm outside of Dallas.

THE ULTIMATE BAD IDEA

In early 1987, the WWF was in complete disarray and business was way down. With Hogan not wrestling at the time, about the only person who seemed to be drawing any crowds was the Ultimate Warrior. But the angle Vince was going with to battle the Ultimate Warrior, Papa Shango, ended up backfiring. Papa's gimmick was using witchcraft to control the Ultimate Warrior and cause him to cramp up, falling to his knees in pain. The Warrior would then roll on the canvas in pain at the stroke of Papa's feathery wand. The match would end with the Warrior spewing green liquid from his mouth as if he was vomiting. Talk about far-fetched! The concept insulted the intelligence of the fans a bit too much.

THE ANIMAL

I have known George "The Animal" Steele for a long, long time. He was very knowledgeable of the business, having served as both a wrestling promoter and talent. Some may be surprised to learn that he holds a Master's degree and has taught in the public school system for years.

Although he never captured any major titles while in the WWF, George was an admirable heel and later got over with the crowd as a babyface. His longtime feud with Randy Savage—in which he fell in love with Miss Elizabeth—is still talked about today. For all his hard work, he was inducted into the WWE Hall of Fame in 1995.

As a practical joker, you never knew what to expect from George. Like all of wrestlers from that era, George protected the business, never letting on to fans that anything was scripted or fake. He had a very unconventional character, and part of The Animal's gimmick was that he couldn't speak coherently. He would just mumble and make unintelligible sounds. So he said very little. But George made up for his silence with some witty humor both inside and out of the wrestling ring.

Some of my funniest stories with George are from the time he was an agent with the company. Part of an agent's responsibility is to critique a wrestler's match. Although we were professional about it, most of the boys would laugh at George's critiques because he really wasn't well known for having the wrestling credentials that would allow him to critique anyone. I know he meant well—and I personally understood where he was coming from—but he just didn't have the wrestling know-how to tell anyone how to wrestle.

For example, during one of my matches I did a leap-frog over my opponent, in which I basically jumped over a standing person. It is a spectacular move and takes precise timing and communication with your opponent. After one match, I was in the locker room when George came up to me to critique the match.

"Tito," he said, "you had a great match out there. The only thing is that I hope you don't do a leap-frog anymore, because when you went up in the air, you were at a slight angle. You weren't balanced and I noticed you leaned toward one side."

I had to do my best to not laugh out loud. The boys and I later had a good laugh at the Animal's expense. Luckily for the sake of my career, I kept doing leap-frogs.

THE BRAIN

Bobby Heenan had been part of the wrestling industry for some four decades. He had done it all, from wrestling, to managing, to TV commentator. When he did the color commentary for the WWF television shows, he regularly insulted me and spoke poorly of me, which was a good thing for me because he was a heel. He did everything possible to help get me over. And he did a great job at it. When he commentated, he said some crazy things: referring to me as "Chico," telling people that "my family and I lived in a 1957 Chevy," and insinuating that fans could always find me "at a taco stand in Mexico." These insults were aimed at helping me get over as a babyface, and they unquestionably did just that. They didn't call him the "Brain" for nothing.

THE ROCKERS

Shawn Michaels and Marty Jannetty debuted in the WWF in 1987 as the tag-team, The Rockers. They were a very energetic and enthusiastic team, and they had great chemistry together in the ring. But they weren't getting the push they felt they deserved, possibly because they were a bit too into the nightlife.

On a plane ride home from a European tour, Marty asked for my thoughts as to why The Rockers weren't getting a shot at the belts. I said, "Look Marty, my only advice to you and Shawn is to sit low and do whatever the company asks of you. Both of you are very talented. When the time is right, and Vince figures out what he wants to do with your tag team, you will get your break. In the meantime, give your best in the ring and watch your Ps and Qs outside the ring. Hang in there, your time will soon come."

A few weeks after we landed, Vince figured out what to do with them when he fired them. About a year later, The Rockers were back in the company, which wasn't surprising. If you had talent, then Vince was a big believer in second chances. Both Shawn and Marty worked as a tag team for the next three years. Then they split as a team, and after feuding against Shawn for a while, Marty was fired shortly thereafter.

I am not sure why things had to change, but I believe that Vince saw something in Michaels. Even though he was very talented, at the time it was considered a big joke by some of the boys because of Shawn's unprofessional behavior in the past. I knew that he had talent and that sooner or later the partying would minimize and he would get focused. And I was right. Today the joke is on the boys, because Shawn is a legitimate superstar.

THE BULLDOGS

As stated earlier, I partnered with the British Bulldogs for a six-man tag match at WrestleMania III. I was especially glad to have the British Bulldogs on my side. Although we lost, I have nothing but good things to say about Davey Boy Smith and the Dynamite Kid. It is widely known that they pulled many mean ribs, but they never gave me any grief—although they had the opportunity to do so. After they stiffed one of their gophers, I confronted them for their shortcoming. The gopher was sent to the convenience store to buy the Bulldogs some coffee. When the lackey returned, they Bulldogs took the coffee but didn't pay him. The guy was upset and for some reason he came up to me for some guidance. I understood his concern and said I'd mention something to the Bulldogs.

"Come on guys," I told them, "after all this guy has done for you two, why not just give him his money. With all the money you are making, you can't even spare a couple bucks?"

They agreed and gave him the money for the coffee as well as some extra for a tip. For a while, I kept looking over my shoulder to see if they were going to pull a rib on me because of the exchange. But, I guess they had enough respect for me because they never looked for revenge, for which I am thankful.

The Dynamite Kid wasn't always so kind-hearted. I am not sure how the feud started, but Dynamite and Jacques Rougeau had a misunderstanding in the dressing room that ended up in a fight that Dynamite pretty much dominated. Unfortunately, the argument led to Jacques leaving the company. He took time off to convalesce, but also to train. Jacques went to the only person who he truly trusted to lead his training, his brother Raymond, a very good boxer in his own right. In the process of training, Raymond taught Jacques how to box.

After about six weeks, Jacques returned to the

company. I am not sure if what followed was premeditated, or if Dynamite was just simply ribbing Jacques again. As the wrestlers were eating lunch together before a TV taping, Jacques went to get his food. The Dynamite Kid was already in the buffet line, and a few words were exchanged. A moment later, Jacques whacked Dynamite right in the mouth with a thunderous punch, knocking out a few of Dynamite's front teeth. Jacque cashed in his receipt and a stunned Dynamite did nothing to further the event. Regardless, Vince found out about the incident and eventually sent both guys home for a while.

Unfortunately, the Dynamite Kid never returned to the company, and I understand today that he is both physically and mentally in poor shape.

GIANT GONZALEZ

Shortly after André the Giant passed away in January 1993, a new giant appeared. Vince brought Giant Gonzalez, an Argentinean, into the league. Giant Gonzalez debuted in February of that year and lived up to the "giant" part of his name. He was a legitimate 7-foot-6 and weighed close to 450 pounds. His height was his original ticket to America, as the NBA's Atlanta Hawks took a flyer on him. But his knees didn't hold up well to the rigors of basketball, and he never played for the Hawks. He was under contract with Ted Turner, so someone came up with the idea of turning him into a professional wrestler.

He had some mighty big shoes to fill in André the Giant. Vince told Gonzalez he would make him a superstar, and to his credit, Vince tried his best. He gave him all kinds of TV build-up, but it just wasn't enough. If you can't produce in the ring, the fans won't support you. Gonzalez just couldn't get it done in the squared circle. His bad knees just didn't allow him much mobility.

THE HITMAN

For many years, Bret was a middle-card worker and he didn't make a lot of money. We often chatted and I always remembered him complaining every tax season that he barely had enough money to pay his taxes. Yet he never complained about his spot. He followed the rules, learned the ropes, and waited for some time before he got his break.

After a meeting in the middle of 1992, Pat Patterson came up to me and said, "Tito, it took a long time for us to decide who we were going to let become the new champion, but you should know that it was between you and Bret. But Vince decided to go with Bret." I was crushed by the news but tried to take it in stride, telling myself that business was business. I personally felt that I had the ability and talent to carry the torch for the company just as well as Bret, if not better. Nothing against Bret, but I had worked a lifetime and was never offered the same opportunity.

In my opinion, Bret should have been particularly

grateful to Vince for the chance to be the world heavyweight champion. At the time, Bret was really just an average worker with a lot of charisma. Initially, it wasn't Bret who got Bret over—it was Vince. With Vince's help, Bret became a very wealthy man. The only reason he was the "best there is, the best there was, and the best there ever will be," was because of the many guys who helped him get over.

THE UNDERTAKER

I can't say enough about The Undertaker, who has been in the wrestling business since 1984 and is still going strong at 43 years young. He has an unprecedented 16-0 record at WrestleManias.

The WWF went on a European tour in 1992, and one of the stops was in Barcelona, Spain. At the time, I was wrestling as El Matador. Since we were in Spain, my gimmick went over well with the fans. In fact, the WWF was so hot in Barcelona, that I wrestled and defeated the Undertaker in front of a record 55,000-plus crowd in the Estadi Olímpic Lluís Companys stadium.

During this time, the Undertaker's character had just started to get a push. Even though I won the matches against him in Spain, I was eventually asked to help get him over, which I gladly did. The Undertaker is a credit to the business, an extremely nice guy who I can't say enough good things about.

The cast of characters poses for a photo opp. at the airport, following a trip to Europe. *Photo courtesy Tito Santana*

HONKY TONK MAN

Hulk Hogan helped the Honky Tonk Man get his break in the WWF. The two had become friends in the Portland territory. Honky had become overexposed in the Oregon area and needed an exit strategy. Like any good

friend, Hulk helped him land an opportunity in New York. Once under contract, Vince gave Honkey his gimmick, an Elvis impersonator, and had him work as a face. Vince then pushed him hard so his character would gain traction with fans, but his character just wasn't catching on. Nothing was working.

Then all of a sudden, Vince changed strategy and decided to make Honkey a heel and give him a manager, "The Mouth of the South," Jimmy Hart. The change worked and the gimmick gained support from fans. Matter of fact, the Honky Tonk Man got red hot.

Honky would later become the Intercontinental champion by defeating Ricky Steamboat. He was a one-time champion but held the belt for 14 months. He told the fans that he was the best ever Intercontinental champion, and he does hold the record for the longest reigning champ.

I never had a problem with Honky and thought well of his character. He left the company after losing the belt in a record 29 seconds to the Ultimate Warrior at the first-ever Summer Slam.

A CLASSY GUY

Pat Patterson was not only a very good pro wrestler, he went on to become an excellent producer and road agent. He was one of the most genuine and straightforward people I ever met. If he said something, you could bank on it. I really appreciated all the advice and guidance that he gave me throughout my wrestling career.

In 1993, the company started to give a big push to Yokozuna, a Samoan-American wrestler who was a simply gigantic human being. He was scheduled to be part of a Battle Royal in Sacramento. I knew the company wanted him to get over as a legitimate heel, but he had very few singles matches under his belt.

When the bell rang, I huddled about four guys together and said, "Let's all four of us make an effort and try to throw the 500-pound Yokozuna out of the ring. But to help him and his gimmick get over, we won't be able to do it. At the right time, I'll call a spot for him and throw all four of us out to the concrete floor at the same time. To show the fans his strength, let's bump real hard for him." Respecting my decision, everyone agreed and the spot worked perfectly. I believe this match proved to the fans that he was a legitimate character and a very powerful man.

Once we were eliminated, I made my way to the back into the dressing room. Pat Patterson took me to the side and, with a smile on his face, asked, "Whose idea was it to do that spot?" I said, "Mine." Pat's smile got bigger and he patted me on the shoulder and said, "Tito, that was a great idea!" Pat's compliment meant a lot to me, and it proved to me that if I ever chose to be an agent in the business down the road, I would probably be able to handle the duties and responsibilities.

11

WRESTLEMANIA RUNDOWN

For my thoughts on WrestleMania I and WrestleMania III, see chapters five and six.

WRESTLEMANIA II

WrestleMania II took place on April 7, 1986 at three separate locations: New York, Chicago, and Los Angeles. I tagged with the Junkyard Dog against the Funk Brothers, Terry and Hoss. (Hoss was actually Terry's older brother, Dory Jr.) In front of roughly 15,000 people in Los Angeles, Terry pinned the Dog after clocking him over the head with his manager Jimmy Hart's megaphone.

It was a wild night because of the unprecedented three-venue pay-per-view. Each venue had its own agents, producers, and announcing team. Our announcing team in L.A. consisted of Lord Alfred Hayes calling the event, Jesse Ventura on color commentary, and Elvira (yes, *that* Elvira, the "Mistress of the Dark") offering special analysis. Keep in mind, part of the allure for WrestleMania was all of the celebrities and dignitaries on hand, helping to bridge the gap to the mainstream. On the night of WrestleMania II, I talked to and signed autographs for many celebrities and their guests, including then-Los Angeles Dodgers manager Tommy Lasorda and actor Robert Conrad.

Although the Dog and I lost the match, I always enjoyed working with the Funks and JYD. Both the Funks—especially Terry—and The Junkyard Dog played a role in the development of my career. JYD went out of his way to help me out when I worked shows in the Mid-South territory. He would loan me his car, feed me, whatever I needed; he treated me like family. I was in awe by his popularity in the Mid-South territory, especially in the city of New Orleans. The town loved him and he was clearly among the most recognized sports figures in the city, even more notable than many of the New Orleans Saints. It is unfortunate that he died way too young in a car accident.

WRESTLEMANIA IV

The highlight of WrestleMania IV for me didn't come in the ring, but outside it, as I met legendary middleweight boxer Sugar Ray Leonard at WrestleMania IV. The event took place in March 1988 at the Trump Plaza in Atlantic City, New Jersey. At the time, I was teamed with Rick Martel as the Strike Force tag team. We lost our match and our championship belts to Demolition that night. In a strange twist, both André the Giant and Hulk Hogan were disqualified in their match against each other for using chairs. Since this WrestleMania was billed as being a tournament for the heavyweight championship, that meant Hulk lost his belt. The Macho Man ended up defeating Ted DiBiase—with a little help from a chair-wielding Hulk—to win the belt.

The locker room was packed with celebrities and special guests. Vanna White was there, but she was coated in make-up and too skinny. I'll just say she looked better on TV than in person. Sugar Ray was the big draw for me. He was a huge professional wrestling fan—despite the fact that he was a lot smaller than all the wrestlers—and had attended many events. I got to know him one on one that night and enjoyed our conversation. He was very impressed with the amount of training wrestlers had to go through and our skill set in the ring. Coming from a champion, those words meant a lot to me.

WRESTLEMANIA V

The fifth WrestleMania was also held at the Trump Plaza. As stated earlier, Martel and I lost to the The Brain Busters in a match that proved a turning point in our careers. Demolition defeated The Powers of Pain to regain the tag-team belt, while Rick Rude took out the Ultimate Warrior to win the intercontinental belt. The marquee match was Hogan versus Savage for the heavyweight belt, which Savage had held onto since the previous year's WrestleMania. Hulk recaptured the championship, which wasn't a popular move throughout the WWF. Some guys sided with Randy and felt he deserved the belt. I disagreed, because at the time Randy was nowhere near as popular as Hogan. It was a good decision by Vince to put the strap back around the Hulk's waist.

When Randy first started in the WWF, the two of us wrestled together. Due to his high-spot wrestling style and preference for aerial moves, the crowds were initially not receptive to our matches. Even though he had worked in other places like Georgia and Kentucky before coming to the WWF, you could tell he was still a relative rookie. In fact, many considered Randy to be nothing more than a curtain jerker, an opening act, when he initially joined the company.

Randy wasn't used to working with top workers or accustomed to the WWF's style of wrestling. His timing was off and he did high-spots just for the sake of doing high-spots. He had to get out of the habit of writing down in advance all the moves that he wanted to use during the course of the match. Wrestling is about impromptu action and reaction. It is an art, and the goal was for us to paint a picture and tell a story. The only thing that any wrestler should need to know prior to a match is the outcome.

Despite these shortcomings, I could still see that Randy had talent as well as a great attitude. He respected the business and he wanted to learn and get better. One night after a match against him in Detroit, I pulled Randy to the side.

"Randy, the fans in this territory like a lot more power moves and mat wrestling. We are giving them too many aerial moves and they aren't responding. Brother, I threw more drop-kicks and arm-drags out there tonight than I have done in months," I told him. "Let's try to go out there in the future and give them what they want. We don't need all these high-spots and drop-kicks."

To his credit, he listened and learned. As Randy worked with the other top guys in the company, they taught him how to work and showed him how to tell a story in the ring. He also improved in interviews with some tutoring. When I was the Intercontinental champion, Randy and I were involved in a program. Even though Randy was supposed to be chasing after me, in his interviews he talked about him becoming the World Heavyweight champion, not the Intercontinental champ. This not only depreciated the integrity of the Intercontinental title, but me, too.

"Randy, you can't talk about getting a shot at the world title when you're supposed to be chasing me," I told him. "Forget about the world belt. Your focus and attention should be on both our match and the Intercontinental title."

He understood, and with patience and practice he improved to eventually become a master at the microphone with a worthy catchphrase—"Ooooh, yeah!" His Slim Jim commercials were priceless.

I didn't help Randy out of preferential treatment, but

because it was the right thing to do. We were a family and fraternity, and each wrestler was supposed to look out for every other. When I first got to New York, I was in the same boat as Randy. Guys like Don Muraco and Greg Valentine took me under their wing and helped me adjust and become a smarter wrestler and better worker.

Little by little Randy was transforming into a better mat worker, but he still wasn't really getting over with the crowd. So in an effort to combat that, Vince came up with the idea to give The Macho Man a female manager, his real-life wife, the beautiful Miss Elizabeth. It was a brilliant move that skyrocketed Randy to the top.

WRESTLEMANIA VI

In a match that had no real buildup or storyline, I lost to The Barbarian at WrestleMania VI in front of 67,000-plus fans at the SkyDome in Toronto. The Barbarian, whose real name was Sione Havea Vailahi, was a nice guy from the South Pacific island of Tonga (where wrestler King Tonga was also from). I thought he was one of the strongest guys in the territory. He had an awesome look and along with his partner, The Warlord, they had a good team gimmick called The Powers of Pain. They never won the tag-team title, but The Barbarian had a long career in both the WWF and WCW.

The highlight of the evening was The Ultimate Warrior's defeat of Hulk, which gave the Warrior the heavyweight belt. Another of the more memorable matches of that evening pitted Dusty Rhodes and his manager, Sapphire, against Randy Savage and Sensational Sherri. The mixed-sexes tag-team match was won by Dusty and Sapphire, with a little help from Miss Elizabeth. I always enjoyed watching Dusty and Sapphire dance in the ring after their matches.

Unlike The Macho Man, Dusty came into the WWF with an impressive track record. He was a booker and a main talent with the Crocket promotion in the South, where he was incredibly popular in the state of Florida. His feud with Kevin Sullivan in the Sunshine state was the stuff of legend. Dusty had lots of charisma and drawing power, and Vince had no problem bringing him to the larger stage in New York.

But Dusty's transition to the WWF wasn't a smooth one. When he signed on, Vince stacked the deck against him in what some saw as an act of humiliation. Others saw it as a challenge. There had been plenty of banter between the WWF and Dusty's promotion in the South when Dusty was the booker there. I think Vince intended to show Dusty who had the power, and that the WWF was the premier wrestling company in the world. So he stuck Dusty in a polka-dotted costume and aligned him with an overweight African-American manager, Sapphire. (Dusty later claimed these were both his ideas.) Many of the boys couldn't believe that Dusty had accepted this agreement.

In my opinion, Dusty turned this negative into a positive. He did what he had to do to work for the number-one wrestling company, and because of his talent, he got the gimmick to work in his favor. He was a great character

TITO SANTANA'S TALES FROM THE RING

and he really understood how to work the crowd. Since he was another West Texas State graduate, I was very proud of him. I enjoyed my time with him, despite the fact that he often roamed the locker room in the nude, which was not a pretty sight. He was a comical guy and he was a credit to the professional wrestling industry.

WRESTLEMANIA VII

My match against The Mountie at WrestleMania VII ended in a disappointing fashion for me, but built a lot of heat nonetheless. In less than two minutes, he pinned me after shocking me with his taser. I would have liked to work the match longer, but I thought the finish made sense to the build up of the night's program.

I have known The Mountie, French-Canadian wrestler Jacques Rougeau, since he and his brother Ray signed with the WWF in the mid-1980s. I thought the pair of babyfaces made a very good tag-team combination. When his brother retired, Jacques took on the gimmick of a Canadian Mountie, the law enforcement officers of the Royal Canadian Mounted Police. I never expected The Mountie to be a good gimmick as a single wrestler, but Jacques was persistent and it worked. He played the role perfectly and drew major heat wherever he went. For him to successfully turn heel was a total surprise.

I didn't mind wrestling The Mountie—when he didn't have access to his taser.

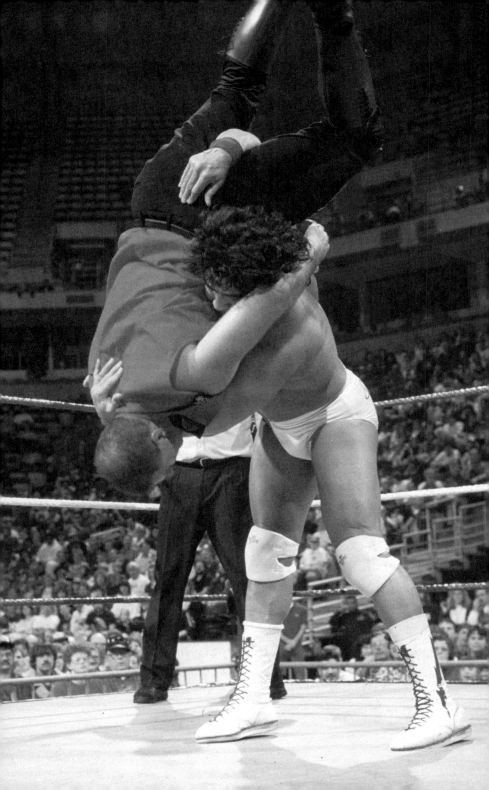

Our match that evening was small potatoes compared to the main event between Hulk Hogan and Sgt. Slaughter. WrestleMania VII was held in March 1991, when the United States was waging war against Saddam Hussein and Iraq. Vince parlayed this reality into a wrestling angle. Despite some negative mainstream press, fan-favorite Sgt. Slaughter turned heel and simultaneously betrayed his country. He spoke poorly of his country and talked of becoming an Iraqi sympathizer. Vince even gave him a manager, General Adnan (Sheik Adnan Al-Kaissy), whose appearance and mannerisms were meant to resemble Saddam Hussein. At the end of a 20-minute match, Hulk beat Sgt. Slaughter to win back the WWF Championship for the third time.

WrestleMania VII was at first supposed to be held as an outside show at the Memorial Coliseum in Los Angeles. However, at the 11th hour, it was decided to move the event to the adjacent, but smaller, Los Angeles Memorial Sports Arena. The company told the media the reason for the venue being changed was that it had received threats from people upset about Sgt. Slaughter's apparent allegiance with Iraq. Whether that reason is credible or not, I think there was another reason: low ticket sales. For wrestling, the Memorial Coliseum in Los Angeles had enough seating for more than 90,000 people. Some of the agents had shared with the boys that ticket sales weren't going so well. The Sports Arena had a capacity of only 16,700 for wrestling. It turns out, WrestleMania VII only drew about 16,200, enough to make the smaller venue appear to be sold out.

To me, the poor attendance had a lot to do with the overdone U.S.-Iraq angle. It was initially a good short-term program, but it quickly ran its course. The Gulf War began in August 1990 and for all intents and purposes it was over in a matter of weeks. American forces won decisively and easily, and the actual war formally ended shortly before WrestleMania. But Vince didn't want to pull the plug on the angle, even though fans had shown some indifference toward it. To his credit, Sgt. Slaughter did a great job with the angle and his character. Yet it was inevitable that the American hero, Hulk Hogan, would eventually win the belt back. Everyone knew it. So why attend the marquee match if the outcome was predetermined?

In my opinion, the company exploited the war. Sgt. Slaughter had come into the company years earlier as a heel and received instant heat because of his ability and expertise at ring psychology. He told me that he was uncomfortable with the Iraqi sympathizer gimmick. Because of the negative heat he initially received from the public due to the gimmick, he had to continuously watch his back. There were some crazy people out there. Fans damaged the cars he rode in and some even made personal threats to him. Still, as a testament to his professionalism, Sgt. Slaughter stuck with the gimmick and made it work.

WRESTLEMANIA VIII

When Vince decided to push Shawn Michaels, he completely changed his boy-band looking gimmick and transformed Shawn into this "Toy Boy" heel character, the Heartbreak Kid. To add heat, Vince assigned Sherri Martel to be his manager. Soon thereafter, I was asked by Vince to help get Michaels over with the crowd as a single's wrestler. I was used as his stepping-stone to championship-caliber matches, and I had no problem acquiescing to the request.

I will never forget our match at WrestleMania VIII in 1992. We were the opening match at the Hoosier Dome in Indianapolis. Even though he beat me in an awesome ten-minute battle, my entrance into the ring was equally memorable. To open the show, country singer Reba McEntire sang a rendition of the Star-Spangled Banner. I was then introduced first to the crowd. As I entered and Rebe left, I extemporaneously kissed her on the hand. It got a big pop and Rebe was a good sport.

My match against Michaels at WrestleMania catapulted Shawn on to an Intercontinental title shot against the champion, Davey Boy Smith. In October of 1992, he beat the Bulldog to win the title. It was the first of many single's championship for the Heartbreak Kid. My only regret is that we didn't wrestle much against each other. He had great abilities in the ring and our styles complemented each other well. I think we could have made a lot of money together.

WRESTLEMANIA IX

My last WrestleMania, the ninth annual event, took place in 1993 at Caesars Palace in Las Vegas. It was held outdoors and featured a wild finish between Bret Hart, Yokozuna, and Hulk Hogan. The Hulkster came away with the championship belt after Yokozuna's manager, Mr. Fuji, unintentionally blinded his own wrestler with salt.

Working the El Matador gimmick, I defeated Papa Shango in a dark match that served as a warm-up for the cameras. I used my "El Paso de la Muerte" ("Pass of Death") finisher on Shango to secure the victory. The finisher was a variation of my usual Flying Forearm Smash, but I would hit my opponent in the back of the neck, rather than hit him in the forehead.

I was the first wrestler in the business to use such a Flying Forearm Smash as a finisher. I created the move, which developed from my years of playing football. I took my knowledge from the gridiron to the air. Television commentators Bobby Heenan and Jesse Ventura helped me get the move over by referring to it as "The Flying Burrito" and the "Flying Jalapeño."

I also used the figure-four leg lock as a submission hold throughout much my career. I started using it in an angle that was created after Greg Valentine broke my leg with his own figure-four leg lock. In the angle, Jack Brisco taught me how to do a figure-four. I eventually returned from my injury to battle Greg Valentine, and used his move to get the best of him.

12

RINGING THE BELL
ON A CAREER

GIVING MY NOTICE

On April 14, 1993, I gave Vince notice of my resignation. He said I was making a wise decision. After all those years, he showed no real emotion about my decision. I thought he would at least express some thanks for a long career, but he didn't.

"Vince," I said, "I think it is time for me to go. I'm not happy and I need to get away from the company for a while."

Vince bluntly replied, "Tito, I think you are right."

I was very sad. I had given myself to the WWF for more than a decade. I just wished that Vince hadn't teased me for so long with the El Matador character, knowing all the time that he didn't have me in his long-term plans. The writing was there on the wall all along, but I was just too pro-company to give up hope. I kept taking the bait like a fool.

I was no longer one of the WWF's top competitors. I was traveling by myself, and the long road trips had become exhausting. Many of the wrestlers that I had socialized and traveled with in the WWF were no longer part of the league. I missed my family and wanted to be home with my children. In short, I was miserable.

After speaking with Vince, I began the drive to the next town where I was scheduled to wrestle. About an hour into the drive, I broke down in tears. It had finally sunk in that I was leaving the WWF. I had no job waiting for me, and no idea how I would make a living or provide for my family. I had not even told my wife, Leah, about my decision. With tears flowing down my face, I struggled to gather my composure. I turned to the one entity that had always been there for me, God. I prayed to God and asked him to do what he wished with my life. To guide me and help me take care of my family. Although the prayer relaxed me temporarily, reality didn't take long to set in: I would soon be unemployed. I would have to share this with my wife.

When the matches ended that evening, I rushed back home to New Jersey. I arrived at the house well after midnight. My wife was asleep, but as usual, as soon as I got into bed, she quickly awakened. As we embraced, she looked into my eyes and immediately knew that something was wrong.

I said, "Leah, I gave my notice to Vince. My wrestling

career with the WWF will come to an end in two weeks. I'm scared and don't know what to do."

"Look Merced," she replied, "for the past decade, Vince has controlled and owned you. You are now free. Don't worry. We will do what we have to do to survive. If we have to, we will sell the house and I will even work extra hours. Please don't worry. Together we are going to make it."

Her words relaxed me and I was genuinely relieved. It was crystal-clear that with my wife's support, we were, no doubt, going to make it.

I had some other business ventures under way to stabilize my income post wrestling. Just a month earlier, I had become a distributor of Quorum Alarms. I'd been reading a lot about the company and its security products for personal, home, and automobile use, and I had a lot of hope of making a good second income for myself.

I also had been putting a lot of effort into opening a Gold's Gym in the New Jersey area, close to my home. My good friend, Paul Alperstein, and I had two locations in mind for a Gold's branch, the Rockaway and Danville area. While Paul and I negotiated with landlords, I talked to representatives from a variety of gym equipment manufacturers. The whole process would cost us in the neighborhood of $150,000, so I was banking on a return from my significant investment. I even got Hulk Hogan to give me his word that he would be at the grand opening of our Gold's. But in the end, the gym did not come to fruition because Paul and I couldn't secure a suitable building location.

WISE WORDS

When I left the WWF, I never looked back. My last couple months in the league were miserable. I hated going to work, but I fulfilled my commitment. I'll never forget my first night home with Leah. As I laid in bed with my wife just staring at the TV, my mind was racing 100 miles per hour. She knew how unhappy I had been for months.

Finally I said, "You know, I'm scared." For the first time since we had been married, I was out of work. We had three kids to support and bills to pay. She looked at me and said, "I'm scared, too, but things will work out. They always do."

I reached over and held her for a while. She pulled away, and looked into my eyes, and said, "You've got your life back. That's got to be worth something."

I let her words sink in before replying, "You're right. We're not quitters. We'll make it one way or another with the help of the good Lord."

The comfort she gave me that night allowed me to get a good night's rest for the first time in many months. I quit feeling sorry for myself and realized that my family was what made my life go around, not the WWF. My three college-educated boys and my wife were what life was and is all about.

GETTING THE CALL

In February 2004, I received a telephone call from Howard Finkel.

"Tito," he told me, "we are going to induct you into the

I enjoyed my induction into the WWE Hall of Fame in 2004.

Hall of Fame. We would like for you to be there and to be part of the show."

The invitation really didn't mean that much to me. I had attended Pedro Morales' WWF Hall of Fame induction in 1995, and I wasn't impressed by the ceremony. It was not the spectacle it has become today.

Howard stressed to me that the event had changed since Morales' ceremony and it was a much more significant occasion. But what convinced me to attend— truth be told—was when Howard told me that I would get paid $5,000 if I appeared in person. I would also be provided limousine service to and from the event for me and my family. So, I said yes.

Howard came through on his promises. I dined at wonderful restaurants and stayed in two luxurious rooms at the Hyatt in New York City. I was given the royal treatment.

To my surprise, the event itself was a completely different program from the one I had attended earlier. There were wrestling fans from all over the world in attendance, and they were not shy about showing their appreciation for me. I was in awe by the many fans from Japan, Europe, and this great nation that came up to me for photos and autographs. I really felt honored.

I was shocked when I found out that Shawn Michaels was going to induct me. Back in the day, Shawn and I had a few misunderstandings outside the ring, none of which turned into much. Still, he was one of the last guys that I would have expected to come out and say nice things about me.

In his speech, he recalled a conversation he had while traveling with Razor Ramon. The pair were chewing the fat as usual when they both came to the realization that they were after my spot in the company. The boys liked the longevity that I had enjoyed in the WWF. I was the only WWF talent to appear in the first nine WrestleMania's, a fact that was not lost on Michaels.

The speech made me realize that a lot of guys had been gunning for my position. At the time, I really hadn't thought about it much. I just worked hard and kept my nose clean. That had earned me a lot of respect from the boys, and from Vince.

In the end, I am glad that I was both inducted into the Hall of Fame and that I went to the event. It made me feel very important, and I enjoyed the opportunity to give something back to the fans. My induction into the Hall of Fame also played a major role increasing my celebrity status among wrestling fans. That led to more independent wrestling bookings, autograph signings and photo appearances, and motivational speaking engagements. For all of that, I am very thankful.

THE FUTURE OF THE BUSINESS

The professional wrestling business has always been around, and will always be around. If anyone believed in us back in 1983, it was Vince. He invested all his money and rolled the dice on WrestleMania I. He was very confident, but he also recognized the gamble he was taking. Well, it turned out to be a great success. The company grew fast, and by the end of 1984, two more pay-per-view events had been added, SummerSlam and Survivor Series. Then came the Royal Rumble. I don't think anyone—even Vince— anticipated that the company would take off as fast as it did.

The straightforward truth about the business is that it is family entertainment. Our business is an art. Some of us are better artists than others. Our matches if done well allow the fans to believe that they are watching two wrestlers competing for an undetermined outcome. There are very few wrestlers who can pull that off in the way it's supposed to be done. Most of those wrestlers are no longer active full time.

Our business has changed so much. When I started in

1977, we had a bunch of different places where we could learn. Promoters kept us around, sending us from one territory to another. We got to learn without being rushed. By the time you were put in a top spot, in most cases you were a polished wrestler and knew what you were doing. As a result, we could sell the sport and protect the business. Fans believed in the reality of our business then; many do not now. Now, it's Hollywood wrestling, promoted hard on TV week after week.

The business has just changed, for worse, from my days in the ring. But it will go on, at least as long as Vince is in control.

GETTING MY LIFE BACK

Now that I am out of the WWF, I feel like I finally do have my life back. Please make no mistake about it, I still enjoy and love professional wrestling. It was and will always be in my blood. Although when I left I had many years left to give to the company, I have no regrets about leaving the WWF. Today, I have the freedom to choose when and where I want to go wrestle. And I do still wrestle because I truly love to perform for the fans. I sincerely believe that without such passionate fans, professional wrestling would have been no more than a passing fad.

I want to remind every fan who reads this book that I am eternally thankful for the support. God Bless you and your family.

Arriba!

ACKNOWLEDGMENTS

I want to thank Terry Funk for not allowing me to give up in the business before I even got started. I am forever appreciative to Andre the Giant and Mario Savoldi for helping me get my start in New York, and for the friendship of the boys, such as Greg Valentine, Paul Orndorff, Lanny Poffo, Bobby Heenan, Rick Martel, and Sgt. Slaughter. I also respect and thank the McMahon family for everything that they have done for my family and me.

Tom would like to thank his wife Janet and son Dante for all their patience and understanding during the writing of this book.

We would both like to thank Noah Amstadter, Andi Hake, Doug Hoepker, and all the fine folks at Sports Publishing for their expertise, guidance, and production with this book.

And the biggest thanks of all go to you, the fan.

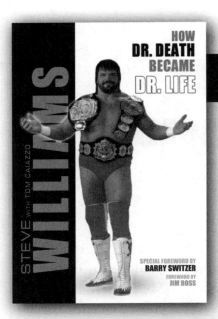

Steve Williams
How Dr. Death Became Dr. Life

Authors: **Steve Williams with Tom Caiazzo**

In this inspiring memoir, longtime wrestling legend "Dr. Death" relives his brawls in the NWA, WCW, WWF, WWE, and Japan. Williams also gets personal, revealing his transcendent journey to conquer throat cancer and discover his alter ego, Dr. Life.

Hardcore History
The Extremely Unauthorized Story of ECW

Author: **Scott E. Williams**

"[Reporting] which will shock not only wrestling fans, but even wrestlers who worked in ECW."
—Wrestling Observer

An honest, in-depth look at the controversial evolution of the ECW, pro wrestling's most bizarre company.

Other wrestling books ...

King of the Ring: The Harley Race Story · Harley Race
An introspective look at one of the biggest names in 1970s wrestling.

Terry Funk: More than just Hardcore · Terry Funk
One of wrestling's enduring figures shares humorous stories from the road and the ri

Dusty: Reflections of an American Dream · Dusty Rhodes
Dusty Rhodes' decisive take on the ups and downs of his legendary career.

Chair Shots and Other Obstacles · Bobby Heenan
All the wit and wisdom of Bobby "The Brain" Heenan.

All books are available in bookstores everywhere!
*Order 24-hours-a-day by calling toll-free **1-877-424-BOOK (2665)**.*
*Also order online at **www.SportsPublishingLLC.com**.*